The Communication Chameleon

How to Lead, Persuade and Influence in Any Conversation

CLAUDIA FERRYMAN

RAINMAKER BOOKS
www.rainmakerstrategies.org
First Edition, September 2011

Copyright © 2011 by Claudia Ferryman
All rights reserved.

For information about permission to reproduce selections from this book, write to Permissions, info@rainmakerstrategies.org

No part of this publication may be reproduced, stored into or introduced into a retrieval system, or transmitted in any form or by any means (electronic, mechanical, photocopying, recording or otherwise) without the prior written permission of both the copyright owner and the publisher of this book.

ISBN: 1466296364
ISBN-13: 978-1466296367

To my family, friends and clients
who graciously allowed me to be a part of their circle,
I am grateful for their questions.
Special thanks to Elisa, for her editorial genius
and for coaching me to the finish line.

ACKNOWLEDGEMENTS

The actual writing of this book began a couple of years ago, when students in my Communication class at the University of Toronto began to ask me if I could write a book so they could share the course with their family and friends. I thank these students for pushing for this book. I'd also like to thank the staff at the University of Toronto who support all my courses; special thanks to Eva. Thanks to Caroline for the introduction.

I needed to capture the content of my course so I started jotting down notes and ideas. Then I hired a film student, Kayla, to film all twelve lectures so that I could review the material visually. I also want to thank Edie and Imshun, who typed up all the lectures and shared them with me.

Over the summer I started writing what became *The Communication Chameleon*, and it soon became obvious that the scope of the book was growing beyond the course material. I recognized that I had to include numerous examples from my business projects in order to illustrate the foundations of the principles that make up this book. The business case studies I included come from my consulting work with corporations and not-for-profit community groups.

I would like to thank all my clients for giving me the opportunity to put my expertise to use. I give special thanks to David, Peter, Nancy, Jennifer, Joanne, Phil, Robert, Nayla, Steve, Keith and Don for their visionary leadership and for trusting me to work with their organizations over a period of many years to develop their human capital. I also want to thank the thousands of employees in the many organizations I have worked with, for putting into practice these tools to great success.

I want to thank my life coaching clients for including me in their journey toward greater well-being. Their stories are an inspiration of human courage. It goes without saying that real names have been changed for all examples in this book.

So many people have contributed extensively to my learning over the years that it is impossible to mention everyone, but know that I am grateful for all that you have done. A nod goes out to my good friends Nick, Henry and Kay, for the great discussions we have had over the years.

I would never have completed this book without the love and support of my family, my encouraging aunties and trusted friends. I thank my mom Vallorie, my first mentor and the person who handed me the original 1936 edition of *How to Win Friends and Influence People* at age nine. No doubt it was one of my primary motivators in becoming a master communicator. Thanks for all the support from my sister Lorice who is always there for me. Thanks also to my childhood friend Christine who has been telling me I can do anything since age ten.

Finally, I want to thank Elisa, who deserves a great deal of credit for this book. She provided the process and the coaching for me to write 70,000-plus words in a matter of weeks. No one contributed more to this book. A gifted writer in her own right, she spent tireless hours brainstorming, organizing, editing, re-writing, laying out and designing what you now hold in your hands. Her assistance is indispensible.

Last but not least, I cannot forget Leo and Sofie, the world's best kitties, who seem to know just the right time to jump on my keyboard or tap me on the shoulder when it's time to take a break!

How to use this book

The book is designed in two sections. The Foundations section is best read from start to finish. These chapters are designed for individual exploration and provide the foundational skills of becoming a master communicator. Section Two, Applications of Effective Communication, can be read in any order and is designed to be referenced for specific applications such as negotiations, interviews, meetings, presentations or effective leadership techniques.

Contents

	Introduction	1

SECTION ONE: FOUNDATIONS

1	The Mind Does The Listening	9
	The Mind-Body Connection	18
2	Reality is Relative	23
3	Emotions Get In The Way (Emotional Hijack)	31
	Emotional Intelligence	36
	Shifting emotional response patterns	42
4	Formative Experiences and Anchors	45
5	Self-Identity	53
	Disassociation	60
6	Behavioural Flexibility/DISC Communication	62
	DISC Communication Styles	64
	Prescription for Improved Conversations	71
	Enhance Personal Relationships	73
	Predicting the Behaviour of Others	78
7	Team Building with the Colours	83
	Communication Do's and Don'ts	88
8	Learning Styles (Representational Systems)	92
	Representation Systems descriptions	96
	Recognizing Learning Styles	102
9	Building Subconscious Rapport	106
	Rapport Building Techniques	111
	Empathetic Listening	120

10	The Importance of Non-Verbal Communication	125
	Reading Body Language	129
11	Conversational Self-Defense	132
	Mental Clarity	140
	Active Listening	144
12	Reframing: A Tool for Change	147
	The Reframing Process	151

SECTION TWO: APPLICATIONS

13	Powerful Negotiations in Seven Steps	157
	Seven Steps to Powerful Negotiations	158
14	Essential Interview Skills and Techniques	182
	Before the interview	182
	During the Interview	199
	After the Interview	203
15	Masterful Meetings	205
	Twelve Steps to More Effective Meetings	209
	Making Powerful Presentations	227
16	Leadership, Influence and Change	229
	Six Principles for Leadership	229
	Motivational Factors	231
	Leadership Styles	238
	Organizational Change Management	246
	Appendix i: Executive Summaries	251
	Appendix ii: Glossary	261
	Appendix iii: References	271

INTRODUCTION

For a long time, a story has circulated about circus elephants. You may or may not have heard it, but it is a great metaphor for why so many people who read books on how to be more effective communicators never really improve. After I share this story with you, I want you to decide whether you will be one of these people, or whether you will count yourself among those ready to embrace the profound changes that they will experience in their lives after applying the tools you are about to learn.

There once was a huge circus elephant that was tied by a rope to a small pole. Everyone wondered how such a small pole and such a flimsy rope could hold the largest living animal on Earth. After all, it would be very easy for an animal weighing over 10,000 pounds to simply tug a little to set itself free. Seeing that everyone was perplexed, the trainer explained to the crowd how such a thing was possible. He told them that when the elephant was just a baby, it was tied with a metal chain to a solid pole. Over and over it would try to free itself, but could not because the chain and pole were too strong.

Years later the chain was switched to a rope, but the older elephant still believed that it could not escape. It had stopped trying. The elephant would now only walk as far as the length of the rope. The boundaries of its world had now become self-imposed.

Like the elephant, we have all experienced the pain of self-limiting beliefs and thoughts. But there are always those among us who are determined to find ways to break free of whatever is holding them back, who differentiate themselves from the pack through their adaptability and willpower to succeed.

The concepts, tools and techniques in this book will provide you with the opportunity to move beyond the behaviours that prevent you from being a masterful communicator. However, to get there you will have to stretch past the boundaries of your comfort zone. And nobody said it would be easy. The change starts within yourself.

I would like to believe that you have a compelling reason for wishing to be a better communicator. Reading a book on the subject will not be enough. This process is intended as a hands-on, multi-dimensional series of steps in which you must be an active participant.

You will be asked to try on new beliefs, break habits and develop new behaviours. There will be exercises, questions and challenges that you'll need to perform to produce visible results. Remember that, as in any other endeavor, you can only get out of something as much as you put in. Do not allow this opportunity to be yet another one of those times when you reached for an answer, grasped it in your hands, but didn't follow through.

You owe it to yourself, to your career and to your future goals, to become the best communicator you can be – and you can accomplish this by learning effective ways for conveying your thoughts, ideas and desires in the most efficient manner possible.

I cannot emphasize enough the fact that the tools offered in this book can only be useful to you if you choose to practice them regularly. Improving your communication skills cannot be an intellectual exercise.

Having shelves upon shelves of self-help books gathering dust does absolutely nothing if you do not apply the techniques they offer you. By putting into daily practice the communications techniques and exercises offered in *The Communication Chameleon*, you will be well on your way to becoming a master communicator.

They say that the first step toward change is awareness. I believe it is also crucial to possess an intense desire for that change. Your desire will always be the motivator that drives you to take action. You can amplify this feeling by visualizing all the benefits you will receive by being able to move smoothly through difficult conversations and subconsciously influence others to follow your lead.

I have worked with individuals, teams and large organizations for over twenty years, helping them to unleash their maximum potential. My clients' results ranged from achieving profound personal transformations, to enhanced organizational effectiveness, to being promoted to their dream job. They didn't start out with any particular advantages over others in their field; in fact, the common denominator in their accomplishments was that they managed to focus on applying the skills you will read about in this book to great success.

If somebody handed you a key that could magically enable you to smoothly navigate every difficult conversation you've ever had, would you not take it? Imagine a world where you can fearlessly ask for a promotion, deal with the demands of a Board of Directors, or sit down for a holiday dinner with your in-laws without breaking out in hives.

Some conversations seem impossible, and often times those are the kind that matter the most. And wouldn't it be wonderful if we could snap our fingers and make all that anxiety go away? If there was some sort of key that could set free our most powerful self?

Many difficult conversations occur because we are unaware of the personal 'stuff' we bring into the conversation. This 'stuff,' which includes our beliefs, emotions, values and formative experiences, influences the way we interpret what's happening in the conversation. We perceive reality from our own perspective and tend to blame the other person for not understanding us.

Truth is, nothing can really stop you from reaching the outcome you are seeking. Nothing other than yourself, that is. Your biggest challenge will be to overcome the tricks your own mind will play on you, and to get beyond the little internal voice that tells you profound change isn't really possible.

The most effective communication requires that you have the behavioural flexibility to accommodate the differences in communication styles of others. This is why I've chosen the metaphor of the chameleon: among the most unique creatures on our planet, chameleons have the uncanny ability to change their colour to blend in and match their surroundings.

In *The Communication Chameleon*, you will be shown how to adapt to any situation in order to influence others to adopt your point of view.

Having excellent communication skills is the foundation of great relationships both in the home and in the workplace.

The Communication Chameleon will guide your development toward communication mastery as you learn how your mind, emotions and physiology contribute to meaningful dialogue. You will learn:

- How to predict and flex to someone's communication style in 2 minutes or less
- The latest in brain research and how it effects communication
- How your mind deletes, distorts and generalizes your interpretation of reality
- When you need to interrupt a pattern of ritualistic conversations
- The behavioural flexibility you need to relate well to anyone
- The underlying reasons why we misunderstand each other during a difficult conversation
- How to overcome emotional hijack and keep your cool during conflict
- Strategic processes for more effective negotiations, interviews and meetings
- Ways to lead and influence others through secret, subconscious rapport-building skills

I invite you to turn the page and begin an exploration of the ways you can improve every relationship of your life. As you learn to identify and revise your internal communication programming, you will experience a powerful transformation. Above all, you will begin to dramatically improve your ability to lead, persuade and influence others in any conversation.

PART ONE

FOUNDATIONS

CHAPTER ONE

The Mind Does The Listening

Let's face it, you don't buy a book about communication unless you're trying to figure out a way to improve your skills of conveyance, networking and persuasion across a wide range of potentially-difficult situations, both in the social sphere and in the workplace. Most people I've encountered in my university communication courses expect to learn techniques for improving their skills; in other words, they anticipate lessons in how to get their interests across effectively in order to make the other party listen better.

When communication breaks down between individuals, the most common tendency people have is to blame the other person for not understanding, while making the assumption that they did their best. This is a very limiting way of looking at things.

The steps and exercises outlined in this book are intended to teach you that the most profound way to improve your communications skills is to learn how to unravel the mysteries of your own internal communication patterns. Gaining insights about your core values, beliefs and perceptions, and how these affect how you interpret reality, is a vital part of deciphering the unknown realms of your subconscious communication pattern.

When you really think about it, there is a lot more to communication than meets the eye. Getting a message through to others is not only about words; it is about the emotions, expressions and subconscious motivations that we bring to the table. We interact everyday in a myriad of ways – we convey dialogue with our facial expressions, our gestures, our ways of interrelating with our everyday world. In modern society we have become so adept at this, that by the time we are adults we've learned to navigate through our world on autopilot, hardly giving second thought to the real reasons why we communicate the way we do.

Many difficult conversations happen because we are unaware of our own 'stuff' – the personal issues that we bring into these conversations, which despite our best intentions can deeply influence the way we perceive what is being said. We can't help but bring our identities and our emotions into the conversation, and most often this is the root cause for triggering difficulties.

To become a masterful communicator, you will need to learn how to navigate your own errors in communication. You will have to become astute at reading others, perceiving both verbal and non-verbal cues, and possess the necessary behavioural flexibility to shift your conversational style to accommodate the person with whom you are speaking.

The first and most basic principle you need to understand is this: **The mind deletes, distorts and generalizes reality.**

Before we can really start delving into ways to persuade and influence others, we need to discuss *how* the mind works and how it affects our perceptual filters. Again, the basic founding block of this principle is the proven fact that ***the mind deletes, distorts and generalizes information.***

Here's a little exercise for you to demonstrate how this works. Quickly read the following words in the triangle below:

```
     Paris
    in the
   the spring
```

Did you miss the repetition of the word "the" twice in the phrase? Glance at the triangle again. As you might have noticed, your mind knows the phase and does not expect to see the duplicate word, so you may literally fail to notice it.

Recognize that the way your mind works affects the way you interpret reality. We know that our perceptual filters are influenced by the mind's interpretation of the stimuli we detect. Our ears hear, but *it is the mind that does the listening*. Our ears may take in what is being said, but it is up to the mind to interpret this information.

We all know that individual interpretations can be a flawed process. A process that can cause us to misinterpret and misunderstand what has really occurred or what we heard. We also know that the mind's ability to create associations is a wonderful shortcut for learning. Yet associations can let us down because we often find ourselves responding to others without even thinking, due to habitual reactions.

If I were to ask you to spell the word SHOP and very quickly ask you to answer the question, what do you do when you get to a green light? Without thinking, you mind has already come up with the word STOP.

This is yet another automatic response that stems from the fact that your mind is in rhyming mode, so SHOP will elicit the word STOP as a response to the question. You might not have fallen into the trap if you had taken the time to be mindful and pay closer attention to the question.

If you've ever taken courses in psychology or brain physiology, you will probably be familiar with the fact that the mind's great capacity to learn so much is due to the process of pair associations and automaticity.

Automaticity is the ability to do things without occupying the mind because the behaviour has become a habit – an automatic response pattern. Automaticity is a form of deep subconscious learning (called subconscious competence) due to the repetition, reinforcement and practice of a specific behaviour or thought.

Compare how you drive your car now, versus when you first learned to drive a car. At some point in time, you must have experienced the feeling that you have driven from one place to another in an almost trance-like state, only to wake up upon arrival. The good news about this kind of cognitive functioning is that, whether it is tying your shoelaces or locking the door when you're coming and going, you have a long list of automatic habits that you can carry out without even thinking. Our great minds are designed for efficiency. However, this efficiency is not always effective when it comes to conversation and communication.

Let us look at the Four Stages of Competency model of learning (developed by renowned researcher and psychologist Abraham Maslow in the 1970s). This model basically stipulates that we undergo four levels of understanding when we are learning something new. They are:

1. **Unconscious Incompetence** is the state where we are *unaware* that we don't know how to perform a task.
2. **Conscious Incompetence** is the state where we are *aware* that we don't know how to perform a task.
3. **Conscious Competence** is the state where we *know how to perform* a task with a lot of *concentration* and active mindful focus.
4. **Unconscious Competence** is the state where *we know how to perform* a task *without thinking*, as described above in the example of driving a car.

Believe it or not, a great majority of everyday communication occurs during a state of unconscious competence. Whether chitchatting about the weather or what we did over the weekend, the process is automatic and we don't give it much thought. The good news is that it is fine to carry out most conversations in this state of mind. Most of us have developed expertise in a specific subject at work, which often requires us to simply regurgitate knowledge. Speaking to our family and friends also takes on a routine style, thus enabling unconscious competence to be very useful most of the time.

How does this serve us when we are trying to navigate our way through an adversarial conversation? How do we negotiate with, or influence someone to agree with our point-of-view? The problem is, these conversations are anything but routine in nature. In a knee jerk reflex, we automatically act the same way we've always acted, and say the same kind of things we have always said, but somehow we expect that the other person will change this time. This gets us nowhere and more often than not gives us the impression that the situation is a dead-end, or tells us that we can't get through to someone because there is something inherently wrong with them.

It's a lot easier to see your boss as a jerk than to figure out a different way of approaching, and enhancing, your interactions.

In times like these, it is more important than ever to actively think of unique approaches. Often, however, we seem to be stuck with the same strategy for responding to these types of situations. Although ineffective, this sort of behaviour can be regarded as unconscious incompetence.

Ineffective communication due to automaticity can severely undermine relationships. I have counseled many couples who, over the course of their relationship, developed a ritualistic style of communication with one another that was responsible for producing this very problem. They find themselves fluently performing the same or similar difficult conversation without giving it much conscious attention.

A large majority of these difficult conversations seem to follow a pattern of triggers and responses. We reenact these **ritualistic conversations** over and over without even being consciously aware of the pattern. Here is an example of a ritualistic conversation.

Four years ago a client asked me to help her improve her communication with her husband because she felt that if things didn't change soon, they would end up getting a divorce. I asked her to describe everything that occurred when she argued with her husband. This included listing all their actions, what they were thinking and feeling, and finally what they said to each other. She explained what happened as follows:

"I arrived home from work and entered the house. Right in front of me on the foyer floor was my husband's jacket – just thrown down. I couldn't believe he had left his clothes on the floor yet again. I yelled, *"Oh no, your jacket's on the floor as usual and I'm not going to pick up after you.*" My husband came into the foyer and started shouting back at me to stop treating him like a two-year old. We continued to shout at each other until I turned my back and walked into the kitchen.

I immediately started washing dishes, clanking pots and pans just to drown him out. Anyway, after the argument my husband just gave me the silent treatment. He did not talk to me for a couple of days. We finally made up when one of us apologized to the other. Unfortunately, this cycle of arguments happens over and over, with us doing and saying the same things. Now it seems to be getting more heated every time we argue."

After reviewing the conversation with my client, I explained that she needed to **interrupt the pattern** in order to break the cycle of the ritual. We discussed how to remedy the situation and decided that the next time she saw her husband's clothes on the ground, she should ask him in a gentle voice why he felt it was ok to leave his clothes on the floor. I also asked her not to walk away and do the dishes as a way to avoid listening to him. She looked at me incredulously, thinking it would be impossible to comply with the remedy. I told her that I knew it would not be easy, but that we would practice.

A technique I use with my clients is to **mentally rehearse**, as well as **role play**, any new interventions or pattern interrupts. We practiced many times; I would ask her to step outside, throw clothes on the floor in the entrance, and then invite her to come back in and so on. After ten repetitions she finally felt she was ready. Two weeks later, she called and said, "Oh my goodness, it worked." I asked her to tell me what had happened.

"The first few times it was like I had no control of my temper, but finally I was able to say to him '*Darling, why do you put your clothes on the floor?*' He looked at me and wanted to know what was wrong with me. '*I'm fine,*' I said, '*I just want to talk calmly.*' My husband then asked if I wasn't going to go do the dishes. Obviously he was still playing his part in the ritual, even though I was actively working on changing my pattern."

Finally, she was able to convince him to sit down and discuss their difficulties. She learned that she made him feel like he was being treated like a kid again, with his mother constantly nagging at him to clean up his room. He remembered telling himself that when he grew up and had his own house he would leave it just the way he wanted. In the end, he was very surprised to learn that he had inadvertently caused his wife to develop "mothering" behaviours because of his own reluctance to clean up after himself. He recognized how unfair it was to keep treating his wife this way.

In turn, she remembered how as the oldest child she was always getting into trouble for not getting her siblings to tidy up their rooms, and how she too had repeated behaviours installed in her formative (childhood) years. Only through a deeper analysis could this couple eventually overcome their ritualistic conversation and move back to a healthier way of relating to each other.

If you think about it, you can probably come up with at least one person with whom you constantly have difficultly conversing. Think about it right now. Who would be on the list? Coming up with one person or one difficult conversation will be important for the upcoming exercise.

Are *you* having difficult conversations that follow a similar pattern as described above? Chart 1: Changing Our Patterns in Communication is similar to the schematic I use to analyze communication patterns in several of my coaching programs. Take the opportunity to complete this chart so that you can review and analyze one of your own ritualistic difficult conversation, then find ways to interrupt the pattern.

Chart 1: Changing Our Patterns in Communication

1. Pick a "difficult conversation" (can be either personal or professional) that you have had, then describe and analyze it in the table below. What were you and the other person saying, doing, thinking, feeling? Look for the pattern of thoughts, emotions and behaviours.
2. How will *you* interrupt the pattern?

	ME	THEM
WHAT WERE WE THINKING		
WHAT WAS SAID		
WHAT WE DID PHYSICALLY		
HOW WE FELT		

Subconscious Communication: The Mind – Body Connection

To illustrate how our mind can cause physiological manifestations in the body, I'll share with you the case of a client who consulted me for help with her recurring anxiety attacks. She first walked into my office looking quite despondent, holding her head down and moving slowly. I invited her to sit on the sofa directly across from me and asked her why she had chosen to see a life coach.

"Oh," she said, "a friend recommended I come see you because she thinks you could help me with my constant anxiety."

I asked her to describe her physical symptoms. She expressed that every Sunday evening for almost an entire year she would experience a series of anxiety symptoms such as irritated stomach, dizziness, a sense of panic, and sleep disturbances. She went on to describe how many nights, right after going to bed, she would begin to toss and turn, breathe shallowly and start to sweat as her anxiety increased. The result was a disturbed sleep that would cause her to head to work in a daze.

I then asked her to describe how she was feeling, and she answered that she felt anxious, panicked and depressed. Finally I asked her, "What are the thoughts or questions you ask yourself at the time the feelings begin?"

She looked perplexed and said this was an impossible question to answer. "I don't think I was thinking anything in particular," she said.

I directed her to close her eyes and replay everything that took place Sunday evenings. Upon reviewing one of her typical Sundays, she started to tell me that as evening approached, she began to think, "What kind of horrible day will I have tomorrow? What if I can't get all the work done? It's always so hectic for me."

In order to get to the root of her anxiety, I asked her to reflect on these thoughts. "What do you think your mind does when you ask yourself this question?

At first she couldn't think of anything out of the ordinary, but with further probing she finally said, "Well, I guess I start to wonder how tomorrow at work is going to work out – will I be able to complete all the tasks on my to-do list, will they leave me alone so that I can focus, maybe I will say the wrong things to my boss…you know, stuff like that."

I asked her how she felt, thinking about these things. "I feel all shaky inside," she said. It was obvious to me how she felt, since as she was describing her feelings she began to display many of the anxiety symptoms that were troubling her.

By deconstructing her pattern, I was able to illustrate to my client that she needed to be very careful about what she thought the night before the start of her workweek, since her thoughts and the questions she was asking herself were directing her mind to see images that elicited her anxiety. She was shocked to realize that just by dwelling on the negative aspects of her job, her own thoughts could cause her to experience the physical reactions she was feeling.

She was finally able to see that the consistent repetition of negative thinking, day after day and night after night, had produced the images that were now manifesting her stress disorder.

I told that she needed to intentionally force herself to shift her thinking in order to create more positive thought-pictures. This was not necessarily going to be an easy task. Her negative thinking had become a habit. Even worse was the fact that every time she had a bad day, it reinforced her belief that her thoughts were correct, which in turn reinforced her belief that her job was indeed stressful. This cycle of reinforcement supported her habit of negative thinking as it got stronger and stronger.

Regardless of the actual stresses of her job, I never tried to convince her that her job was not indeed stressful. But through our sessions together, she now understood that by focusing *only* on the stressful aspects of the job, her mind was amplifying the degree of stress.

We become victims of our own negative thinking by self-fulfilling them through our perceptual filters, which have been attuned to look for and recognize only those things that prove right our beliefs and thoughts. My client saw that she was locked in this vicious cycle of beliefs, which determined how she was filtering her situation, and finally provided the "proof" of her beliefs.

She now recognized how her thoughts and behaviours had enhanced her stress levels. The good news was that by understanding her contribution to her own stress, she could now reverse some of the affects and break free by taking control of these very thoughts and behaviours.

Begin to reflect on how many times you too have focused on the negative aspects of your situation, only to produce more of the feelings you DON'T want. The mind is a powerful tool that is designed for problem-solving. As you direct your mind by choosing the questions you ask yourself, the mind will immediately go into action to find the answer, even if the answer causes you anxiety and panic.

Imagine a mother who panics whenever her children leave home, because all she can think about are all the horrible things that might happen to them. When I tell her that she needs to imagine them coming home safe, she resists – she feels justified due to all the negative things she has heard on the news. She tells me, "I *have* to be worried," and resists shifting her thoughts.

Of course it isn't easy to simply put an end to the thoughts that create negative results in our lives. We typically have experiences, reasons and justifications for why we hold such thoughts. Yet when I asked this mother to choose between a life of panic and worry, or a life where she could have a peaceful state with practical precautions to make her children secure, she finally chose to take charge of her worrying habits.

Hopefully by now you are also convinced to start reviewing how your mind might be deleting or distorting reality and thereby causing you to communicate in automatic, ritualistic ways. Take a close look at how you are directing your mind through the questions you ask yourself.

The Prescription

> If you are suffering from anxiety, can you pinpoint what thoughts might be contributing to the cause? Could it be habitual negative thinking? Are you troubled by any persistent thoughts which you now suspect might be causing you physical symptoms? Take this opportunity to review your thoughts.
>
> Physical symptoms (anxiety) that I can attribute to negative thinking:

List the habitual thoughts you should work on changing:

The new thoughts I choose to replace the habitual ones:

CHAPTER TWO

Reality Is Relative

Imagine that you and a friend have just left a party. On the way to your car, you talk about what the hostess was wearing. You both agree it was a red dress, but this is where the agreement ends. You say the dress went below her knees and your friend says it was just above her knees. You believe that it had a lace collar and your friend says it was embroidered. It's obvious that you and your friend's perception of what you saw don't match.

It is very important to understand the concept of perception because it dictates how we will behave and respond in all areas of communication. **Perception** is the process in which we interpret and organize stimuli to understand and give meaning to the experiences we are having. In other words, perception is the process by which sensory stimulation is translated into experience.

Our perception of the world is primarily based upon how we process the sensory input from our eyes, ears, nose, tongue and touch. It is well known that what we perceive is often different from what might really be going on. There are multiple factors that affect our perceptual filters, including the situation / setting, the other person, and the perceiver's own mind.

In this discussion we want to focus on you, the perceiver. Your attitudes, motivations, values, interests and experiences all affect your perceptual filters. Your perception of *reality* is *relative* to who you are and how you view the world. We create our own reality by choosing what we focus on. The object of our attention is given greater importance in our subjective reality. We end up with **selective perception**, where we selectively interpret the behaviour of others based upon our particular interests, experiences and background. As a result, many misunderstandings may rise between people due to **perceptual errors**, which are a common barrier to effective communication.

A simple example of how our personal preferences affect perception can be seen when we examine what we are focusing on at any given moment. Have you noticed that the last time you bought a car or had your eye on a specific colour of car, you begin to see the same car or colour everywhere you go? How can you explain this phenomenon? Did everyone suddenly buy the same car you want? Obviously not, but your purchase of that vehicle begins to influence where you are directing your attention. Consequently, you are more likely to notice things that are top-of-mind – in this case, other cars like yours. Here we see how our internal mindset can affect our perceptions. We discussed earlier that our minds deletes, distorts and generalizes information, and now we see another way our mind can play tricks on us by skewing our view of reality.

I had a client who really wanted to test her perceptual filters, so I suggested that she conduct a mini experiment. Just before she left my office, I asked her to pick something on her way home to focus on, and to see if she could notice it more than usual throughout the week. A week later she arrived for her next session all excited to share what had happened. She told me that on her way home she was cut off by a Volkswagen Beetle on the highway. She decided to choose this car to focus on for the rest of the week.

By the end of the week, she was shocked at how many VW Beetles she'd seen. She noticed them in her favourite parking spot at the mall, behind her in traffic, in driveways and parked on the street. Virtually everywhere she turned, there was another VW Beetle.

On the way to her next appointment, she decided to see how many more cars she would spot before getting to my office. She turned onto a street and right there in the driveway she saw not just one, but three VW cars. The story gets even more peculiar because there were an old, a new, and a toy VW Beetle all sharing that driveway. She sat there dumbfounded, considering how weird it was to see all these cars in one spot. What were the odds? How often had she passed this driveway without noticing these cars? Weird indeed! She was an immediate convert, no longer holding any doubts that her perception was highly subjective.

We know that when you put your attention onto one thing, you filter out other data. My client couldn't tell me what other brands of cars were parked beside the VW Beetle – she only saw what she directed her mind to see. We know that this high level of attentiveness to one thing will definitely cause us to miss out on other important facts, but what would your life be like if you had to pay attention or process every single piece of stimuli that you encountered?

While you are trying to focus on a task, you would notice the whirling of the fan, the birds chirping outside your window, the crickets in the garden, the street noises, the people taking in the other room, the hissing of the coffee maker, the TV flickering at the corner of your eye and the person walking by your desk. Your mind would be so bombarded with the many sounds and images, you probably wouldn't accomplish much.

We are fortunate to have a part of the brain that takes on the role of gate-keeping to help us focus our attention. This is called the **Reticular Activating System**, also known as the RAS. The reticular activating system helps mediate transitions from relaxed wakefulness to periods of high attention. The RAS is made up of billions of nerve cells that are densely packed at the central part of the brainstem. The RAS helps us focus by screening the type of information that is allowed to get through to the conscious mind, while filtering out other stimuli. We are spared from having to process all the background "noise" by screening these out, as the RAS gives us the bandwidth to pay attention to only certain messages.

We know that the selective perception described here can cause us to misjudge others. When we are having a conversation with someone, we immediately begin to take in bits and pieces of what we are seeing and hearing because we cannot take in everything. But the bits and pieces we take in are not randomly chosen – we are accessing our previous experiences with that person, along with our own interests when we select what to focus on.

This type of perceptual processing is designed to assist us in quickly reading a situation, but depending solely on this could cause us to experience inaccuracies. To illustrate this point, imagine that you overhear a rumor that your company might be bought out by another. You might attribute the new visitors who are meeting with the general manager today to being part of the acquisition team, when in fact they might just be new clients or personal guests.

Perceptual processing can also cause us to be susceptible to judging the behaviour of others based upon our own biases, expectations or past experiences.

Misinterpretations in communication can come from any of these types of judgments.

Let's say that you invited someone out for lunch and they declined to go. You tell yourself they refused because they don't really like you. Just imagine how you would behave towards them the next day at work. Quite possibly, without consciously planning to, you may begin to behave awkwardly and be aloof around them. They, in turn, will feel put off by your behaviour – with the end result being that they start to treat you similarly. Both individuals will avoid each other and on the cycle will go on and on, damaging the relationship even further.

If we expect something, we begin to act as if what we expect is real, as seen in the example above. This is a great example of a **self-fulfilling prophecy**. Self-fulfilling prophecy is a term used to describe the phenomenon where an individual works toward the validation of what they perceive, expect or believe. Humans have a great desire to behave consistently with how others perceive them, which is also another aspect of self-fulfilling prophecies.

Suppose that the person refused lunch because they already had made other plans and it had nothing to do with you, but your response toward them (due to your feelings of rejection) caused them to begin to really dislike you. You can imagine how often conversations go off the rails because of our self-fulfilling expectations or distorted perceptions.

> *Can you think of an example where your expectations caused you to make a mistake in your interpretation of what was happening? Once you review the situation, can you see how your values and preferences might have warped your perception of reality? Write down your answer.*

The Prescription

Whenever you have a disagreement with someone about what has occurred in a particular situation, it is likely due to a perceptual error at the root of the faulty interpretation. Stop yourself before you blame the other person for not seeing things the way you do. We now know that people can perceive and describe what they see happening quite differently, but this doesn't mean that one person has the right interpretation and the other person is wrong.

You should encourage everyone involved in the conversation to listen to each description of the occurrence before making a final conclusion of what happened. It is very likely that each of you will gain a fuller picture of the situation. Communication is an interactive process of moving information back and forth, with all parties striving for understanding.

Pretend that you are in the other person's shoes. Sometimes I might, quite literally, sit in their chair or move to another spot in the room so I am not anchored in my own perspective. Can you see how they came up with their point of view? When someone says or sees things very differently than me, I am always intrigued about the reasons why they think, feel or see things the way they do. Are you genuinely curious about why people see things differently than you do?

People bring their past experiences and judgments into a disagreement, so before making any assumptions you should review what you know about them. When you encounter differences of opinion, your recourse is to actively listen and engage the other person in deciphering each of your individual perspectives to determine where there might be a common thread. Discussing each other's background assumptions and expectations can help you to better understand why you might have such different interpretations of a situation.

To open a dialogue about different perspectives, begin by saying *"It appears that we are seeing things differently. I know it's natural, since we have different experiences with this subject. I would like to take some time to understand your perspective and review where I'm coming from on this."* Alternatively, you could ask questions to clarify points of dispute, such as *"Can you help me to see how you came up with this by reviewing some of the background information?"*

I remember taking a friend out for dinner and she insisted on just having the soup and salad even though I wanted to treat her to a steak or seafood platter. Initially I was annoyed and began to insist that she choose something else, but she wouldn't budge. I finally decided to have the soup and salad as well. As we ate, I was determined to figure out why she would not have a more substantial dish.

When I asked her again why she didn't go for a lobster, she calmly said, "My parents had been through the war where they had to ration everything and growing up they taught me to never take advantage of a friend by wasting their money. I really value our friendship and so I felt strongly about you not spending too much on dinner."

For a second there I wondered if she meant I was spending money frivolously, or I couldn't afford it. But I had to catch myself and realize that we were coming from a very different place, so I shared my perspective on the situation.

"That makes sense to me", I said. "I grew up with parents who would encourage us to give our guests the best of what we have, even if you had to spend a bit extra to do so."

Developing your ability to navigate the many different perspectives you will come across is a crucial aspect of gaining a better understanding of other people and their inner perceptual processes. This will lead to much richer and meaningful conversations where differences are appreciated rather than a source of frustration. These differences can enhance your relationships, creativity and innovation.

CHAPTER THREE

Emotions Get In The Way (Emotional Hijack)

Today's modern workplace has many psychological dangers which can cause us to experience a great deal of emotional crisis. We have more to do in less time; colleagues are in competition with us for scarce resources; the economic situation has us fearing for our jobs. These are common examples of external stressors. Many of my clients over the past few years have been looking at transitioning their careers because the work they are doing feels meaningless and irrelevant to them, creating a constant internally-driven stress.

But what is the root of that stress? The answer may surprise you. Deep within our brain's temporal lobe there is an almond-shaped mass of nuclei called the *amygdala*. This part of the brain plays a primary role in the processing and storage of our emotional reactions. When we feel fear, the fear stimuli is processed by the amygdala, where they are associated with memories of the stimuli and a fear response is elicited.

In other words, we experience fight or flight symptoms along with the accompanying emotional responses when we are stressed. We might feel a rapid heartbeat, freeze up and breathe shallowly as stress hormones are released – all being reactions we would naturally experience if we were under physical danger.

This creates a state of emotional hijack in which we are ruled by our physiological response.

When we perceive stimuli that might be stressful or fear-producing, such as someone's negative tone of voice or a reproachful look from someone in a position of authority, the amygdala takes over and often causes a typically-irrational reaction while the logical, rational part of the brain fails us.

This fear reaction essentially hijacks our higher thinking, leading us to interpret the situation in ways that dramatically skew our perception of reality. Our emotions grow out of control and we become hyper-sensitive to what is happening around us. This is emotional hijack. Thinking becomes muddled and confused when we experience intense emotions. The possibility of misinterpreting what's happening becomes very likely.

Take a moment for self-reflection. What are some of your external and internal stressors that might be causing your emotional hijack?

My external stressors are:

My internal stressors are:

A client visited my office recently to discuss an interesting example of emotional hijack at work. He indicated that his boss would often ask him at the last minute if he could stay late to help finish up reports. A number of times he missed all or parts of important family events because of these requests. When he had first started working there, he didn't mind complying since he wanted to make a great impression so his boos would understand his great work ethic. Six months later, however, it became clear that his boss was not going to change this behaviour.

Nowadays when his boss asked for something, my client just nodded and stormed away silently, feeling angry. By the time he arrived home he was very short-tempered with his wife and kids. He had already tried to give his boss a hint with non-verbal communication (shrugging his shoulders, grimacing and holding his head down), but his boss noticed nothing. My client now felt helpless to change the situation since his boss appeared to think it was ok to give last minute projects all the time.

As we reviewed the situation, I asked him if he had ever told his boss that he couldn't keep staying late at work on short notice. He answered, "No, I can't find a way to tell him." I told my client that a lot of time had passed without him addressing his boss's behaviour, so the boss had probably come to regard such expectations as reasonable and would continue to make last minute requests. In reality, his boss probably hadn't even realized that such requests were unreasonable since his employee had never objected.

My client needed to see that by not speaking up and explaining that it was stressful for him and his family when he stayed late on short notice, he had contributed to his own problem. By not speaking up he had shown implicit compliance. By freezing up and not explaining, he was creating his own emotional hijack. His inability to speak up and make clear how he was feeling is a typical flight response. Instead, he would internalize his dissatisfaction and behave irrationally with his family.

So what was the remedy to his dilemma? We reviewed and rehearsed what he would say to his boss the next time such a situation arose. Like in earlier examples, this was a clear-cut case where my client needed to "interrupt the pattern" he had established with his boss. Naturally, he was very nervous about what his boss' reaction might be if he was to refuse his request.

We discussed his concerns in depth. He had to understand that his behaviour toward his boss didn't have to be automatic. It had become automatic for him to just say yes, and now it would take conscious effort to stand up to his boss and say no to similar demands in the future.

I advised him to discuss the matter with his boss prior to another request to stay late was made, because it would be much more difficult to break the pattern during a request. In other words, breaking the pattern in his case would require that my client become assertive and approach his boss well before another request is made.

The next day, my client asked his boss for a brief meeting just after lunch (a good time to have conversations because the person is more likely to be in a "satiated" state). He started by thanking his boss for taking a few minutes out of his busy day, then took a deep breath and repeated what we had rehearsed.

"I feel responsible for misleading you about my short notice availability. For the past six months I would readily agree to stay late on short notice, even on days when I've made plans with my family, and I never told you that it was becoming more and more stressful to keep breaking plans with them.

I realized that I've been more and more upset about this. I really enjoy working here and with you, and I don't want this to affect how I feel. I am hoping we can work together to plan ahead for the days you will need me to be here a little later, and this way I get back my work/life balance."

When he recounted his story, he said that the entire time he was speaking with his boss, his hands were sweating and he felt nervous, but the more he expressed how he felt in a very relaxed but assertive way, the more relieved and confident he felt. When he was finished he stayed silent and waited for his boss' reaction.

To his surprise, his boss apologized for taking him away from his family and said he had not realized his employee was stressed. They both committed to be more forthcoming with each other about how things affected them. His boss said that he would definitely work with him to improve timing and plans for project tasks so that he would have as much lead time as possible.

My client was very grateful that his boss was so understanding about the situation. He was shocked that he hadn't said something earlier and let things get to that point. He finally realized how important it is to address behavioural issues early on, so a pattern does not set in and expectations get muddled. He also acknowledged his implicit compliance with his boss' demands through his own "flight behaviour."

Many of us can certainly relate to this example. How many times have you avoided addressing the behaviour of someone who has caused you to feel upset, because of your own flight behaviour or fear of conflict? Have you ever walked away and blown up much later, causing the person to be surprised that you were even upset, rather than calmly and assertively letting them know that you were affected negatively by what they had said or done?

We often fear talking about our feelings, especially in the workplace. We don't want those around us to think we are unprofessional or too emotionally sensitive. So, we don't bring our feelings to work. But these days we have discovered that *emotional intelligence* is essential for worker effectiveness at all levels in the organization and is an important consideration for promotion.

Emotional intelligence (EI) can be defined as the ability, skill, and a self-perceived ability to identify, assess, and control the emotions of oneself and others. The roots of emotional intelligence can be traced to Darwin's work on the importance of emotional expression for survival and adaptation. In 1920, E.L. Thorndike used the term social intelligence to describe the skill of understanding and managing other people. Similarly, in 1940 David Wechsler described the influence of non-intellective factors on intelligent behavior, and further argued that our models of intelligence would not be complete until we can adequately describe these factors.

In 1983, Howard Gardner introduced the idea of multiple intelligences, which included both interpersonal intelligence (the capacity to understand the intentions, motivations and desires of other people) and intrapersonal intelligence (the capacity to understand oneself, to appreciate one's feelings, fears and motivations). In Gardner's view, traditional types of intelligence, such as IQ, fail to fully explain cognitive ability.

Despite the variance in theoretical approaches, all these researchers shared a common principle – traditional definitions of intelligence are quite lacking in their ability to fully explain performance outcomes and the promotion-readiness of individuals. All models also share a common core of basic concepts that include Self-Awareness, Self-Management, Social Awareness, and Relationship Management.

The model introduced by Daniel Goleman in 1998 breaks EI down into a wide spectrum of competencies and skills that drive leadership performance. Goleman's paradigm outlines four central EI constructs:

1. **Self-awareness** – the ability to read one's emotions and recognize their impact while using gut feelings to guide decisions.
2. **Self-management** – involves controlling one's emotions and impulses and adapting to changing circumstances.
3. **Social awareness** – the ability to sense, understand, and react to others' emotions while comprehending social networks.
4. **Relationship management** – the ability to inspire, influence, and develop others while managing conflict.

Each construct of EI has its own set of emotional competencies within. To Goleman, emotional competencies are not innate talents, but learned capabilities that must be worked on and can be developed to achieve outstanding performance. Goleman asserts that individuals are born with a general emotional intelligence that determines their potential for learning emotional competencies. (Boyatzis et al, 2000).

A large portion of the work I do requires performing assessments for staff on their core competencies and their EI, and then creating a plan for development. In my experience, individuals can improve their EI if they are willing and actively work on building self-awareness.

The term **emotional literacy** has commonly been used interchangeably with the phrase "emotional intelligence". Emotional Literacy was used first by French psychotherapist Dr. Claude Steiner, who defined it as "the ability to understand your emotions, the ability to listen to others and empathize with their emotions, and the ability to express emotions productively.

To be emotionally literate is to be able to handle emotions in a way that improves your personal power and improves the quality of life around you. Emotional literacy improves relationships, creates loving possibilities between people, makes co-operative work possible, and facilitates the feeling of community. (Steiner, 1997)

Steiner believes that at its core, emotional literacy is about understanding your feelings and those of others to facilitate relationships, including using dialogue and self-control to avoid negative arguments. The ability to be aware of, as well as read other people's feelings, optimizes one's communication skills and enhances their interactions with others, in a phenomenon that Steiner describes as "emotional interactivity". By looking inwards rather than focusing on one's social setting, Steiner argues that personal power can be magnified to transform relationships in all areas of life, professional and personal.

To summarize, emotional literacy can be broken down into five parts:
1. Know your feelings
2. Have a sense of empathy
3. Learn to manage emotions
4. Repair emotional damage
5. Put it all together = emotional interactivity

Growing research literature suggests that EI may play a far more important role in career success and job performance than general intelligence (cognitive ability). Recent studies have shown that emotional intelligence is a better predictor of a person's suitability for promotion than pure intelligence.

A meta-analysis of 69 independent studies explored the predictive validity of emotional intelligence with diverse job performance outcomes (Van Rooy, 2004) and found correlations that suggest EI can be considered a moderate predictor of job performance and success, relative to other types of personnel selection techniques – including interviews, personality inventories and assessment centers.

Other recent EI research studies suggest that:

- Highly conscientious employees who lack social and emotional intelligence perform more poorly than those high in conscientiousness and emotional intelligence.
- On average, strengths in purely cognitive capacities are approximately 27% more frequent in high performers than in the average performers, whereas strengths in social and emotional competencies are 53% more frequent.
- The highest performing managers and leaders have significantly more "emotional competence" than other managers.
- Poor social and emotional intelligence are strong predictors of executive and management "derailment" and failure in one's career.

Given the solid body of research that has been produced over the last few decades, it is clear that EI is not something that can be overlooked or neglected. If we want to succeed in our personal and professional ventures, we must increase our emotional intelligence in order to be better at expressing our emotions in a calm, constructive manner.

The Prescription

Why is emotional hijack and emotional intelligence so important to understand in effective communication? As discussed earlier, past emotional experiences and our reactions to them are stored memories in the amygdala part of our brain; as such, these past emotional events might cause you to react to the present as if you were actually re-experiencing the past. Even if the present situation is only an approximation of the past, you might still find yourself recycling your response, which is most likely inappropriate to the present event.

Typically when we try to express emotions, we might say something like "You made me angry when you said I wrote a bad report." The problem with this statement is that that it instantly creates defensiveness in the other person. It sends them right into their own emotional hijack and renders them unable to reason with us. In addition, by using the word "you", you blame the entire person for your emotional reaction, which is somewhat inaccurate and makes it impossible for them to figure out what they specifically need to change to make things better.

The other person may have triggered a negative emotion within you, but you still have a choice in how you will respond. Mostly we react by expressing our emotions in a non-constructive way rather than in a **relaxed, assertive** manner. To be relaxed and assertive means that you are in full control of your response, and you are mindfully expressing yourself. Recognize that you may or may not get acknowledgement from the other person, but you do not need to be afraid to assert a clear boundary around how you wish to be treated.

As an alternative, you could say "When you used that tone of voice and said the report was bad, I felt disrespected."

Let us deconstruct this message to illustrate why it is a more accurate of expressing how you are feeling. First, you have **identified the specific behaviour and words** that caused you to feel disrespected, this makes it easier for the other person to change. Also, you have **owned your emotion** by saying "I felt", which is another way of coaching yourself to also own the reaction. **Relaxed-assertive** means that you have expressed yourself in a controlled state which can lead to a **constructive conversation** where the other person is less defensive and thus more able to really hear what you are saying.

Overcoming physical responses

A constructive conversation is only possible if you and the other person are not under an emotional hijack. But what happens if you are already under emotional hijack? What do you do to get out of it?

If you remember, we discussed earlier that when we lose emotional control over a situation, we are experiencing not just the stressful emotions, but also undergoing a flight-and-fight response which impacts our physical feelings and reactions. Thus, when encountering a stressful situation, we need to immediately do something to overcome both the physical and the psychological effects of the emotional hijack. Here is my recommendation. First, think about the physical experiences you might have when you are angry: a flushed face, holding your breath or clenching your teeth. Until you reduce the effects of these symptoms, you will not think clearly.

The first step toward alleviating these physical reactions is by taking a few deep breaths and focusing on moving your conscious attention into your body – relax your muscles, unclench those fists and teeth.

A tip I often give my clients is to wiggle their toes inside their shoes, and to walk away or silently count backwards from 100 until they regain sufficient emotional control. Such activities go far toward reducing nervous-system reactions and bringing us back to higher levels of thinking where we are rational and sensible.

Shifting emotional response patterns

Once you have overcome a negative physical reaction, you must direct your attention to your feelings. Over the years I've learned that it is impossible to have a rational conversation if you have not acknowledged and validated the intense emotions that are present.

People want to know that you understand how they feel before they are able to move on. The second step in overcoming an emotional situation is to listen and acknowledge the other person's feelings and to express and validate your own.

One way to figure out how others are feeling is to ask, "Can you please share with me how you feel about this situation. I really do want to understand what I can do to make things better." By inquiring into another person's feelings, we might find out that they are upset about the specific words we have used, our tone of voice, or something we did physically. These are all behaviours we can work on changing.

We can express our apology for how the other person feels. However, it is important to distinguish between our feelings of empathy because someone is hurt, versus agreeing with their perspective on why they are hurt.

Imagine that someone has unintentionally done something to hurt you. You respond by raising your voice or using unkind words because you feel hurt. Rather than helping the situation, your emotional reaction becomes a distraction in the conversation, because now the other person feels justified for being angry. By yelling at them, the focus has moved away from their behaviour to yours.

In this situation, we can be sorry for raising our voice and apologize without having to agree with the other person or condone their behaviour. You need to make an attempt to clarify the difference, and you can do so by saying: "I am sorry that what I said hurt you. I apologize for raising my voice AND I do want to discuss how I was also hurt by what has happened."

Is it easy to control our emotional reactions?

No. I am the first to admit that emotional control is not easy, especially if you have an established pattern of response with a particular person which leads to the ritualistic conversation we covered in an earlier chapter. However, by building up your self-awareness, you can begin to catch yourself before you repeat the behaviour you desire to change.

It is important to be patient with yourself as you start to make these changes. Automaticity is working against you. You're working against the grain, fighting back against the impulse to reach for the familiar, and duplicate a set of behaviours that are not doing you any favours at present. But naturally your subconscious wants to repeat the programmed response. When you catch yourself slipping back into such a pattern, gently remind yourself to

STOP the old behaviour. Then immediately fill yourself with the new behaviour that you are substituting for the old.

Below is a summary of steps you can use to interrupt negative emotional patterns.

1. Develop self-awareness of your own emotional pattern through self-reflection, or by asking family and friends to help you to notice the pattern
2. Catch yourself just before, during, or even after performing the old response
3. Tell yourself that you have chosen to STOP this behaviour. This will cause you to subconsciously pay more attention to the ways you tend to react.
4. Deal with the physical symptoms of the fight-and-flight response by breathing deeply, walking away, counting backwards or wiggling your toes
5. Immediately catch yourself and mentally rehearse or act out the new behaviour
6. Practice the new pattern over and over until it becomes automatic

CHAPTER FOUR

Formative Experiences and Anchors

Communication mastery begins with the conversation you have with yourself.

Our formative experiences contribute to the main components of our core belief system. These beliefs become the foundation of how we interpret external stimuli and perceive our reality. Many of our subconscious habits and aspects of our self-image are laid down during our formative years – and by this I mean not only our developmentally-formative years (birth to age ten), but also the first encounters that come to form the foundation of our belief system – the friends we have in school, the social and community groups we belong to, our first love and our first job.

We already know that many of our everyday reactions to stressful situations, as well as patterns of behaviour, can come up automatically, without any need for thinking. Our mind is efficiently designed to take in as much information as possible and store it for future use without the need for us to process it all. These subconscious patterns can work for us or against us, depending on whether the resulting behaviour is constructive or destructive.

Several years ago, a client came to me to help her overcome once such subconscious pattern, what she called her addiction, to a well-known Canadian coffee shop chain. Every time she drove past one of these shops, she instantly felt the urge to drive in and buy a coffee. Over time she became very concerned about the amount of caffeine she was consuming every day, so we worked together to design a hypnotic script that would have her substitute herbal tea for coffee.

After three sessions of hypnosis, she began to see results. Now each time she entered this coffee shop, she would order herbal tea. However, she began to experience another peculiar behaviour every time she bought the tea: she would ask to have a lot of cream added, just like when she had ordered the coffee. She realized that she didn't use to have any cream or milk in her tea, but now that she no longer bought coffee, she really craved the cream.

As she relayed this behaviour to me, I instantly recognized that her addiction was actually to the cream rather than the coffee. I asked her, "When did cream become so important to you?" She looked at me in a puzzled way. "What do you mean?" she asked. I repeated, "Think back, when did eating cream become significant in your life?" She suddenly burst into tears and told me the following story.

Growing up we used to receive fresh milk in bottles that were left at our door step. I would race home ahead of everyone else so that I could scoop the cream off the top of the milk and eat it. It was so delicious and it was all for me. I would feel so good, peaceful and safe for about a half-hour before my siblings and parents came home. My dad was an alcoholic and when he came home at dinner time, there was always fighting in the house. He would shout and swear at my mother and all of us children.

I informed her that the cream had become **anchored**, or connected to the feeling of being safe and at peace. Whenever she felt any stress pop up in her life, her subconscious guided her back to the cream to recreate these positive feelings as a coping mechanism. In essence, the cream was the stimuli and the response was the happy feelings she gained as a result. It became clear to her that she needed to find ways to create positive feelings without having to consume large quantities of cream.

Through additional sessions she gained further insights into how her formative experiences were triggering many of her reactions to others, including her sometimes angry outbursts. We worked together as she developed a number of new behaviours and responses that helped her to manage her stress and not turn to old patterns for comfort.

Let's take a closer look at what happened here. We see that formative experiences can subconsciously drive our behaviour without our knowledge. These past events create associations between a specific event and a particular state of being.

In this case, when stressed as a child my client started pairing the eating of the cream with the positive emotions of being in control, feeling peaceful and safe. Many years later, her stress retriggered the association, and she reached for the cream. A typical stimulus-response pairing was now in charge of her actions. Stimuli-response pairings are triggered by **anchors**. In this case, the anchor was the stress my client was feeling, which triggered the need to relieve it by consuming cream.

I witnessed another powerful case of anchoring in a client whom I will call Jim. Jim was referred to me by a good friend with whom I had worked with many years earlier. Jim told me that whenever he went to parties, he would suddenly develop very sad feelings. He had thought about it many times, but could not determine what would cause this shift in his emotional state. He would be having a great time, when out of nowhere he would get hit with a sense of overwhelming sadness.

I asked him to replay, step-by-step, the most recent party he could remember attending where he had this emotional shift occur.

"Well," he said, "I remember we were all sitting around in my brother's backyard, just having beers and burgers and chatting. An old family friend arrived and walked around just shaking hands, saying hi to everyone. When he got to me, he gave me a friendly tap on the shoulder and ask how things were. As I began to tell him how great everything was, I could feel a shiver go up my back. In no time, a wave of sadness was running through me. I got up to leave soon thereafter, but my brother stopped me and asked why I was leaving so early. I did what I always do when I make my escape – snap at him to let me go, and tell him I was too busy to stop and explain myself."

Jim continued to describe how this cycle of sadness – becoming short-tempered, then snapping at others – was a standard part of his communication repertoire, especially with his family. He really wanted to figure out what was going on so that he could repair his relationship with his brother and other family members.

I knew that I needed to look for the anchor that was triggering his reaction. He described over another event, and I started to notice a common thread. In each case there was a moment where someone would tap him on the shoulder. I asked him, "Do you remember a time in the past when you were tapped on the shoulder, over and over again?"

He looked perplexed for a moment. "Why would you ask me that?"

I responded by asking, "Why, do you remember something?"

Tears suddenly began to stream down his face. He said, "Yes, I remember being 14 years old and sitting in the foyer of our house. Everyone who came in walked over to me, tapping me on the shoulder and saying, *Sorry about your mom, everyone misses her but it will be ok*." His mother had just died and this was the reception after the funeral.

After Jim composed himself, I showed him how being tapped on the shoulder was associated with the sadness he was feeling at that moment; essentially, the tapping became an anchor. Nowadays, every time someone tapped him on the same shoulder it brought back the sad feelings, particularly during a party-like atmosphere where family and friends were present. The combination of the setting and the tapping were triggering his emotional shift, which in turn caused him to snap or completely shut down and stop communicating with the people around him.

Jim had not fully completed the grieving process for his mother and the sadness was suppressed, only to surface when triggered with the tap on the shoulder.

The Prescription

Jim and I worked together to successfully replace the anchor. Replacing an anchor involves a technique called **"squashing the anchor."** In Jim's case, the anchor was both unknown to him and unintentionally created to elicit a negative response (anchors that are unintentionally created are called *natural anchors*).

Therefore, to squash the anchor we needed to intentionally create a new, powerful positive anchor which would be used to counteract the negative one. We did it by tapping him on the opposite shoulder, while asking him to remember many positive memories in order to get him to reach an ultra-positive emotional state.

The process then required that both anchors be triggered together. This meant tapped him on the left and the right shoulder simultaneously, so that over time the positive feeling would neutralize the negative one. Triggering both anchors initially caused Jim to have very mixed feelings, but after several applications the tapping of the left shoulder no longer produced sensations of sadness. Jim also worked on bringing closure to his mother's death.

We have illustrated how our formative experiences contribute to our programmed subconscious behaviours. It is vital to gain a clear understanding of how your past has embedded subconscious anchors that trigger specific reactions in you. Then look at how they are related to your interactions with others.

We have observed the importance of our formative experiences and anchors as a way to learn more about ourselves and the subconscious processes that drive our behaviours when we communicate with others. On your road to discovery, you will gather an inventory of triggers and situations that might lead to difficult conversations. There are a variety of tools that can help you to break free of such deeply-ingrained negative habits. I have already written about *pattern interrupt* and *squashing anchors* as great tools for breaking habits.

Anchors can also be intentionally set to be used to your advantage. Physical cues can be utilized to interrupt a pattern and elicit a more positive, desired state. Here are a few examples:

- **Example 1:** Every time you dance, snap your fingers when you are in a positive state. The snapping fingers will become an anchor to being in an excited state. The next time you feel a bit down or tired, stand up, take a deep breath and snap your fingers to rekindle the euphoria.

- **Example 2:** Do you remember seeing people who are just about to meditate clasp their thumb and index fingers together as they sit cross legged? The clasping of the fingers is the anchor toward a calmer state. You too can create a resourceful anchor for creating a calm feeling. In order to set this anchor, touch your fingers ever time you're in a relaxed state. Soon you'll discover that whenever you want to initialize this peaceful feeling and release positive, calm emotions, all you have to do is touch your fingers together.

Some people habitually and subconsciously make a certain movement with their body when they are in a particular emotional state. Observe how someone behaves when they are happy: what are their habitual gestures? You can build rapport – a positive connection – by imitating this habit. You might just cause them to jump back into that happy state.

I have seen an example of this with a salesperson with whom I worked in the past. He would always rub his hands together whenever he got excited about a pending deal that he was about to close. He was totally unaware of this subconscious habit. Any time I wanted him to get excited about a new project, I rubbed my hands together just like he would and my action triggered him to do it too, making him very excited about working on the project.

Finally, you can also create an anchor for yourself to help you get into an advantageous emotional state. If you are about to attend an important interview or negotiation and really want to jump to a more energetic state, select a body movement that inspires you to get excited, such as snapping your fingers. Snap your fingers many times while imagining that feeling of excitement. This will create the anchor. Just before you enter the meeting, snap your finger several times and feel the excitement rise within you.

Can you think of a behaviour that seems to come out of nowhere and totally takes control of your mind, your emotions and your actions? Can you figure out if there is an anchor that triggers this response?

Take a moment to list a couple of these types of behaviours and the circumstances behind their formation.

Behaviour 1. How do you think it was formed? Is there an anchor?

Behaviour 2. How do you think it was formed? Is there an anchor?

CHAPTER FIVE

Self-Identity

So far we have seen how our mind, our emotions and our formative experiences effect our interpersonal communication. You have probably acknowledged how much effective communication depends on your level of self-awareness. But there is one more aspect to explore to round out the picture – our self-identity.

Conversations are among the most primary ways that we use to express who we are in the world. We use conversations as a means to ensure that we come across in a manner that is consistent with the image we have of ourselves.

Our self-identity, also commonly termed as self-concept, is our internal multi-faceted model and understanding of the 'self' as it relates to a number of characteristics such as gender, intellect, race, skills, abilities, competencies, physical characteristics and the personality we've identified for ourselves. Self-knowledge of our identities is enhanced by our self-awareness, and is impacted by our self-esteem. We are continually self-assessing ourselves and applying labels such as good, bad, lazy, and other such qualifiers.

A person's self-concept may change with time as reassessment occurs, which in extreme cases can lead to an identity crisis, or when we are confused or hurt about new revelations uncovered by what people say about us. Furthermore, self-concept is not restricted to present information; it includes past selves and future selves. Future or possible selves represent individuals' ideas of what they might become, what they would like to become, or what they are afraid of becoming. They correspond to hopes, fears, goals, and threats.

The pioneers of the study of self-concept are renowned psychologists Carl Rogers and Abraham Maslow. Rogers believed that everyone strives to become more like an "ideal self." The closer you are to your ideal self, the happier you will be. Rogers also claimed that one factor in a person's happiness is unconditional positive regard for others. Unconditional positive regard often occurs in close/familial relationships, and where we maintain a consistent level of affection regardless of the recipient's actions.

Arguments can often leave us feeling disturbed about how we appear to others. Will they think we are unstable, mean-spirited or unreasonable? Our identity is threatened if people say we are any of these things, because we don't want to believe negative things about ourselves. We want to feel worthy of love, recognition and attention; appearing as a positive and valuable person is essential to our self-image.

Unraveling our inner workings and gaining knowledge of where we have vulnerabilities in our self-identity is the best way to arm ourselves against behaving in ways that cause us to become off-balanced. If we have foreknowledge of the extreme tendencies we have inherited from our experiences, we can avoid acting in inappropriate ways.

Many of these tendencies could be considered *defense mechanisms*, which we use to protect our identities. We also need to develop an understanding of the signals we subconsciously send out through our behaviour, language and attitude, which create difficult interpersonal interactions and conversations with others. Could you be attracting contentious relationships because of unknown vulnerabilities?

You have probably encountered people whom you have to address in a particular way (i.e. handle with kid gloves) otherwise they might react explosively. They appear hypersensitive to the simplest things you may say to them. It is possible that these individuals are suffering from a mental illness such as depression; however, I have found many individuals who are driven by subconscious aspects that push them to respond in this manner. This chapter covers examples of various individuals who underwent a period of self-exploration to reveal aspects of their self-identity which they felt were detrimental to themselves and to their relationships. They wanted to shift their abrupt communication approach and release the pent-up emotions that often caused them to behave in a destructive manner.

I recently worked with a client who came to me to deal with his pattern of attracting women who, according to him, played hard to get. Whenever he became interested in someone, she turned out to be inaccessible or just rejected him. Worse, he'd had a difficult childhood where his mother was detached and rarely expressed her love.

I have seen this pattern emerge in other clients who keep trying to capture the love of the person who is a representation of the parent they most wanted to receive love from – the parent who they feel abandoned or rejected them. In this client's case, this situation manifested in the form of the unattainable women he met in his life.

He constantly repeated the pattern of trying to win their love, only to end up with more heartbreak.

Essentially, his subconscious believed that if he could get these women to love him, he was metaphorically replacing the love of the parent who rejected him. His attachment to his self-identity as the nice guy was not helping him to connect with others who could appreciate him. The women he dated primarily took advantage of him. Yet, due to his low self-esteem and a desire to please, he believed that he would eventually convince them to stay with him.

His pattern defines a situation of many who have experienced rejection by a parent in childhood. We idolize an absent or neglectful parent because the child had to hold onto a belief that his parent has to love them in some way. But the obsession to recapture this love translates into an unreciprocated attraction to individuals who represent the idolized parent.

The alternative might be to reject this parent by not wanting to be like them. As such, we reject their qualities within ourselves. We judge and reject people who represent the characteristics of the neglectful parent, and we do so by developing a push-pull within ourselves – instead of integrating these aspects (our shadow selves) by accepting that we too have the capacity to be like those we idolize or reject.

When we accept our shadow selves, we take charge of the forces that drive us toward the type of people who are symbolized by the past, individuals whom we can never truly win because the whole fantasy is built upon an illusion.

Another example comes from a female client who found that she was attracted to men who were emotionally shallow, womanizing and uncaring like her own father, who had walked out on the family for another woman when she was 15 years old.

She wanted to know how she could be attracted to someone so similar to the father who had created so much pain for her family. Why was she drawn to uncaring men who would just use and reject her? While she was acting out this pattern, she actually did not realize that she pursued men who were similar to her father. She failed to see how her subconscious expectation was that if she could win their love, it would be just like gaining the love she'd always wanted from her dad.

In our sessions, she judged and criticized her father harshly for being disloyal and abandoning the family. She was even more confused when she realized that she was tempted to act in ways which were similar to her father's behaviours. Over and over again, she acted out a "rejection signature" by behaving in a cycling pattern – either unfairly rejecting people in her life or allowing herself to be rejected by choosing to be with people who were never able to commit. She also found herself critical of her spouse and was constantly attracted to other, archetypal men who personified her father's characteristics.

Could she accept the fact that she was capable of the same actions as her father? Could she too become disloyal to her spouse? The way she was finally able to navigate through this addiction was by accepting that indeed, she did have the capacity to be just like her dad. Her lifelong rejection of him was also a rejection of aspects of herself. Now that the subconscious motivations were out in the open, they would no longer drive her actions without her cognizant awareness.

I asked her to consider that these rejected aspects of herself could be seen as her shadow self. She needed to examine this shadow and to accept the truth that would be revealed, even if negative feelings of shame and embarrassments might emerge.

> **EXERCISE: Figuring Out Your Shadow Self**
>
> Make a list of people you feel highly critical of. List all the characteristics that push your buttons, and then answer the following questions:
>
> What are the characteristics you are judging or criticizing about this person?
>
>
> If you had that behaviour yourself, how would it make you feel? Why do you think you would reject it in yourself?
>
>
> Reflect on past actions where you have put yourself down. What negative things did the little voice at the back of your head tell you about yourself?

As you work toward unlocking a greater understanding of yourself you become a better judge of character, which will come in handy when you attempt to read and persuade other people's motivations. Seriously examine the possibility that whatever qualities you reject in others may be a reflection of what you fear most about yourself. You need to be open to looking at all aspects of 'self' in order to see things as they really are, rather than be affected by wishful thinking.

Naturally, acceptance does not mean expression. Acknowledging that you share similar qualities with someone you dislike does not imply that these qualities will manifest the same way in you. You are a unique individual. As you go through life, you attract experiences that help you explore the things you reject within yourself. As you resist, reject, judge or criticize any attribute in someone else, it is possible that you might become more attracted to it subconsciously, and/or manifest it through destructive behaviours of your own.

When we repress whatever we cannot accept about ourselves, we build an internal void. This surfaces as hurtful behaviour towards others, such as angry outbursts that destroy healthy communication.

One client told me that she found herself addicted to "sad stuff." When I asked her what she meant, she said that she would start to imagine how her young cousins would feel if their father left them, and how they would end up with "messed-up lives". She reflected on how everyone would then understand her and why she had had a difficult life because her father left. Her little visualizations eventually led her to feel guilty and sad about wishing a negative consequence on someone else just so that she could prove a point.

In fact, she was creating scenarios where she disassociated and could **re-witness** these painful events without feeling the intensity of her own feelings. In the end she still experienced a dose of sadness; it was as if within these small doses of sadness she was slowly re-experiencing the great sadness of losing her father. Each visualization helped her witness the pain from an outsider's perspective. This is a process known in psychology as *disassociation*.

Disassociation is a powerful technique for helping us to re-evaluate and **reframe** the events in our life by viewing them from different perspectives. Often in disassociation we project onto others the feelings that reside within ourselves but we cannot confront or accept.

In psychological **projection**, we deny our own feelings and subconscious characteristics but assign them to someone else. Projection reduces negative feelings by allowing the expression of the unwanted unconscious impulses without letting the conscious mind recognize them. One type of defensive behaviour that can be considered psychological projection is *blaming*.

Blaming others is one of the primary defense mechanisms frequently used during confrontation. We are more comfortable trying to figure out what the other person did wrong, rather than looking at their own contribution. We want to avoid the discomfort of owing up to our faults, so it is easier to blame the other person for creating the disagreement. In essence, we project the faults onto those around us and remain unconscious of our own weaknesses.

We may find ourselves testing people who are closest to us. This is a common tendency: *"Let's see how much of our crap they will take before they reject us; if they keep putting up with it, they must really love us."*

We self-sabotage our opportunity for happiness by pushing them away our loved ones with these tests. The natural consequence is we begin to feel guilty for hurting our family and friends. It is a form of self-punishment, where as we ill-treat those around us, they react with self-protection or defensiveness and in turn reject us. The more we act out this relationship pattern, the more it becomes reinforced until it becomes a habit, automatically being triggered by the most inane circumstances.

We develop an unending cycle of inflicting pain and feeling guilt. To deal with it, we create justifications for why we behaved the way we did, get angry again and finally re-inflict the pain. We are trapped and hostage to repeating the same cycle again and again. I call this the **cycle of revenge**, because we feel justified in exacting retribution for all the wrongs we perceive to have experienced.

As you're reading the examples in this chapter, you might recognize similar patterns in yourself or others. You might also be wondering if people can really change parts of their self-identity in any real permanent way. The answer is *Yes*, people can and do change. It starts with a burning desire to have more harmonious relations with others.

Awareness is the first step toward meaningful change. Then you must choose to change. Choose to forgive or apologize. Choose to let go. Then take action. Do the exercises outlined in this chapter and throughout the book. You will soon begin to break unhealthy habits, thereby reducing the affects of the guilt, frustration or the anger 'button' being pushed. Taking charge in this way means having a great deal less conflict in your life. This is your reward for exploring aspects of your self-identity and reconciling underlying triggers that cause you to behave in non-constructive ways.

CHAPTER SIX

Behavioural Flexibility using DISC Communication Styles

Behavioural flexibility is the single most important aptitude you will need to develop in order to achieve communications mastery. In today's diverse society, you must become a chameleon in how you communicate.

As individuals we are very comfortable in our natural style of communication, so much so that we take this same approach with everyone. The reality is, the person we're speaking with has their own unique communication behaviours, which may or may not correspond with your approach. For instance, we personally might like to keep the conversation high-concept, avoiding details, but the person we're talking to might need to hear details in order to get into the dialogue. As great communicators, we need to flex our approach to best suit the style of the other person.

We have discussed the importance of developing **behavioural flexibility**. This is defined as the ability to shift our behaviour and communication style based upon the situation and the person with whom we are communicating. Behavioural flexibility is possible if we first understand ourselves and simultaneously have a process for reading others. We must figure out who is across the table from us so that we can anticipate how to communicate with them.

In order to flex to others, you must have a system of predicting how people will behave. For the past fifteen years, I have used a communication model to help individuals understand their style and the style of others. This model is also useful for team building and leadership development programs. It is called the DISC Communication Model, which is a powerful framework designed to help read observable behaviours that depict a specific communication style.

DISC is a system of psychological assessments that was developed by John Geier, an American psychologist who based his work on the research of another American psychologist, William M. Marston. The founding blocks of the DISC Communication Model were derived from Dr. William M. Marston, who in 1928 wrote a book called *Emotions of Normal People*. In it, he described four primary emotions and the behaviours people have when expressing one of these emotions.

Many models have since been developed from his original theories. Marston viewed people as having passive or active attention, depending on the person's perception of their environment as being either favourable or antagonistic. He devised the following four quadrants to describe people's behavioural patterns:

- Dominance factor will produce activity in an antagonistic environment
- Inducement factor will produce activity in a favourable environment
- Submission factor will produce passivity in a favourable environment
- Compliance factor will produce passivity in an antagonistic environment.

This model was called the Universal Language of Behaviour, and focused on specific observable behaviours in specific environments. The four styles are possessed by all individuals and occur in order of intensity, with one factor being strongest, then the next and so on. The strongest factor would be considered to be the primary or natural style, and dictate the preferred behaviour of the individual.

The specific DISC model I will introduce here was developed based upon Marston's model by an organization in the United States and described in *The Universal Language DISC* by Dr. Bill Bonnstetter and his associates. In this schematic, DISC corresponds to four primary factors:

- Dominance (referred to as Red) – relates to control and strong assertiveness
- Influence (referred to as Yellow) - relates to social connections and conversations
- Steadiness (referred to as Green) – relates to patience, predictability and thoroughness
- Compliance (referred to as Blue) - relates to structure, procedures and analyzing

We will look at each of these factors to gain an understanding of our communication style and how we can predict the communication style of others so we are able to modify our approach to best suit them.

The Dominance Factor (Red)

The Dominance factor is highest in individuals who are very direct and get to the point in their communication style. They are **extroverted**, **assertive** and impatient when communicating with others because they know what they want and would like others to get to the point. We will call these the Red communication style. Reds don't want to deal with a lot of details when you first begin speaking to them. They prefer you to tell them where you are taking the conversation by first summarizing the objectives. They want to be convinced that you are organized and thorough with the backup material that supports your case.

Reds are highly **task-oriented** and always appear to be in hurry. They are not shy to take risks to accomplish what they want. They believe that you need to try things and not wait until you have a perfect solution, because things can always be improved along the way. Constant movement toward task completion is necessary is their philosophy. To listen to Reds speaking, you would find out that their magical words are *time*, *results* and *"get to the point."*

Most Reds can be considered **external processors**, this means that they like to think out loud. They process information and ideas through dialogue. It is not uncommon for Reds to sort through a problem by talking about it out loud with a respected colleague. They want to control the conversation and will usually take charge of its direction by asking questions or stating their opinions quickly and succinctly.

The Influence Factor (Yellow)

The Influence factor is highest in individuals who want to converse in a casual, social manner. They believe that daily social connections are essential, and they feel better having these interactions throughout their day, even if they are working on an unrelated task. We call these types Yellows, who are regarded as the conversationalists of the DISC styles. Yellows are **people-oriented**, as opposed to Reds who are task-oriented. Like Reds, they are also **extroverted** and **assertive** and like to engage in discussions with others about ideas and opinions. When you have a conversation with a Yellow, you will find that they may jump from subject to subject and from one idea to another. This can cause frustration for others, especially those who prefer to stick with one topic from start to finish (such as those with a high Steadiness and high Compliance factors).

Yellows are also **externally processing**, preferring to brainstorm aloud and generate multiple high level solutions to problems. They are not as focused on the implementation of these ideas as someone who has a high Steadiness factor, or even a Red who is keen on getting things done to see tangible results. Yellows love talking it through and stating their opinions without interruption. You might find it is hard to get a word edgewise when they are on a roll.

As discussed, Reds and Yellows are extroverted profiles. **Extroverts** have a tendency to be gregarious and assertive, and are the first to introduce themselves in a room full of strangers. They are not shy or afraid to be in novel situations where they are required to be outgoing.

On the opposite end of the continuum are introverts. **Introverts**, in contrast to extroverts, are individuals who appear to be more reserved and introspective. At a party full of strangers, an introvert prefers to stand back and observe the scene, waiting until someone else approaches them for an introduction. Introverts, although appearing shy, may just be more selective in the number of social interactions they choose to engage in.

Steadiness Factor (Green)

The other two factors in the DISC model, Steadiness and Compliance, are both introverted profiles. First we will discuss those with a high Steadiness factor, whom we'll call the Green style. Greens are soft-spoken individuals who have a keen focus on those around them. They are **people-oriented**, just like Yellows, and are accommodating and personable.

When you communicate with a Green, their preference is for you to make a connection with them through a personal comment and/or a friendly hello before you get down to the business at hand. A Green is **less assertive** compared to Yellows and Reds, and will take their time to warm up to someone through a careful observation of that person. Greens are **internal-processing**, which means that they will think things through before speaking up.

I invite you to imagine how a conversation about a report would go between a Red and a Green. As opposites, you can imagine the potential difficulties that might arise from their interaction. The Red will want to get to the business at hand and immediately start talking about the report, ignoring the small talk the Green wants in order to make a social connection prior to discussing the report. Each side is focusing only on what they want out of the conversation.

Compliance Factor (Blue)

The final factor is Compliance. Individuals who score high on the Compliance factor (Blues) are typically highly detailed, focused and non-assertive. Like Reds, they are

task-oriented, with a desire to stick strictly to business when at work. They are seen as serious and precise analysts who want nothing to do with idle chit chat. Blues focus on thoughts, not feelings, while they work through the details of a situation, analyzing each piece of fact thoroughly. They want others to be accurate in the information they are providing when in dialogue. Vague or general statements are seen as shallow, if not supported with the appropriate data.

Blues are **internal processors**, like Greens. A Blue can remain very quiet in a conversation. They will deliberately weigh each word and statement before replying, while also waiting for the other person to stop talking so they can think things through.

Determining Your DISC Communication Style

Extraversion and introversion were first used by Carl Jung, a Swiss psychiatrist who was very influential in a number of areas in psychology that include Analytical Psychology, dreams, the unconscious mind, and psychotherapy. He wrote about the concepts of introversion and extraversion in relation to the one's physic energy. Dr. Jung felt that when a person's energy flows outwards they are an extrovert, and when the energy flows inwards the person is said to be an introvert.

Carl Jung further stipulated that extroverts feel a surge of increased energy when they are in the company of others, but experience a depletion of their energy when on their own. Conversely, introverts feel energy lost in large groups of people and energized when they are alone.

> Think about yourself! Are you an introvert or an extrovert? Do you feel energized or depleted in large groups? Circle your answer below.
>
> I am an extrovert
>
> I am an introvert

Now think about whether you are more task-oriented or people-oriented. We know that task-oriented people don't want to be interrupted when they are working on an activity. These are individuals who are very comfortable sitting at their desks alone, locked away from all the distraction of having to interact with others.

People-oriented people are not bothered by others dropping by their desk for a quick chat while they're working. They welcome the interaction, which can often stimulate or energize them for the next step they have to complete.

Now let's figure out your DISC Communication's style. The four factors can be seen as follows:

High Factor	Colour	Extroverted/Introverted	Task or People Oriented
Dominance	Red	Extroverted	task-oriented
Influence	Yellow	Extroverted	people-oriented
Steadiness	Green	Introverted	people-oriented
Compliance	Blue	Introverted	task-oriented

By now, you should have a good idea of your colour and which factor is highest for you.

> Write your colour and high DISC factor below:

The following diagram depicts the four colours as four quadrants around a circle. This is a valuable tool for quickly visualizing the colours and the high level attributes of each, so that you can easily remember the framework. This will be important for recognizing different styles when you begin to use the system to predict the behaviour of others.

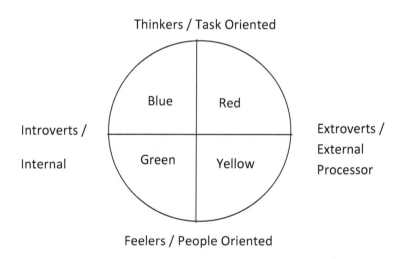

A Prescription for Improved Conversations

External Processing vs. Internal Processing

Earlier, I illustrated how Blues or Greens, as internal processors, will take their time to listen and review what you say before they speak up. Imagine a Blue or Green speaking with a Red or Yellow external processor. Reds and Yellows could find the nature of internal processors a bit disconcerting since they might wonder why the Blue or Green person is not contributing to the conversation.

Think about how this frustration would build as a Red or Yellow person keeps talking, hoping that a Blue or Green will respond. Meanwhile, the Blue or Green will be waiting for the Red or Yellow to stop speaking so that they can internally process the conversation in order to come up with a response. Notice that neither side is getting through to the other.

What do you do in this situation? Red and Yellow individuals who are self-aware and flexible will pause to give the Blue or Green a chance to think by saying *"I've been doing a lot of talking, let me give you a chance to reflect on what I have been saying."*

When giving instructions, external processors have a tendency to jump around as they think aloud, which is confusing for an internal processor. Therefore, Red or Yellow individuals should always leave the door open to give the Blue or Green person the opportunity to come back to clarify information or instructions.

They could say, *"Now that we have gone through the instructions for the report, I know that I have a tendency to only cover the high level steps, so if there are details you might need to know when you carry out the task, so feel free to check back with me for clarifications."*

Self-aware and flexile Blues and Greens will know to ask for time to process by politely saying to a Yellow or Green, *"I would like to contribute to the conversation, but I just need a moment to reflect on what you're saying."* Blues and Greens need this time to think things through, and should rightfully ask for it. An internal processor needs to keep track of all tangents made by an external processor, and at times during the conversation take time to paraphrase and summarize the information.

More or Less Details

Reds and Yellows are less detail-oriented than Blues and Greens. If you have to convey a large amount of details to Reds and Yellows, it is best you provide them in writing. Extroverts become overwhelmed if you begin to drill down too deep into the details too quickly in the conversation. Stick to a high level discussion and follow-up with a summary plus all supporting data.

Conversing with Blues and Greens requires that you provide lots of data to support your case. Don't be shy to give them a step-by-step outline of your information, discussing any details as you go along.

Our DISC profiles include all colours, in varying intensity. Usually there is one colour that is stronger than the rest, and it becomes our **natural style** – our preferred way of relating to others. Typically there is also a second colour that stands out, and it is considered our **adaptive style**. It is not uncommon to behave one way at home and then shift our behaviour at work. These changes can usually be seen as a shift between our natural and adaptive style, depending on the environment we are in.

In developing behavioural flexibility, we have a duty not only to flex to the other person, but also to ask for what we need in communication. We can achieve a perfect balance of all factors if we take the time to perform a situational analysis and shift according to who and what we encounter.

Task-oriented vs. People-oriented

In order to understand why each DISC styles have different practices in completing work versus socializing, it is important to contrast a task-oriented Red or Blue versus a people-oriented Yellow or Green. Reds and Blues want you to stick to business and avoid personal anecdotes. Yellows and Greens want you to make a friendly, personal connection before you start talking about the task. So remember to break the ice with a Yellow or Green and to get right to business with a Blue or Red.

How The Colours Can Help Enhance Personal Relationships

Having an understanding of colour styles can help you facilitate more effective communication in your personal relationships. I have helped many couples through difficult times and often have found a breakdown in communication at the root of their issues. I utilize a DISC Relationship model assessment, which has served as a vital tool in diagnosing core communication problems among couples.

A year ago I assisted a couple who had been referred to me by previous clients. They both felt that their life together was unfulfilling. The majority of the time they argued with each other, and they complained that their relationship was mundane and lacking in intimacy.

In our first meeting I recognized a pattern in the arguments they were having. The wife felt that her husband did not care about her because whenever they argued he would sit silently and say very little. She had to do all the talking and he contributed very little to the dialogue. She would become more and more upset since he appeared to shut her out and often shrugged his shoulders and walked away from the conversation.

He, in turn, felt that his wife wanted to force him to talk about things before he was ready. She would approach him and fire off many questions, and before he could even respond she started to accuse him of not caring because he never said anything. He felt that things always escalated to the point where he felt that he literally couldn't think anymore. His only choice was to leave the situation, which he knew would make her more upset, but felt that if he stayed he might say something he would regret.

Do you see the pattern? The wife is an external processor and the husband is an internal processor. While the wife wants to talk things through and express her emotions, the husband wants to reflect on what she is saying before he speaks up.

We explored the fact that since the wife was a Yellow, she found it easy to express her feelings, whereas her husband, as a Green, would need sufficient time to process his emotions. Instead, he was getting overloaded with the content of the communication to the point where his mind shut down. He wanted his wife to understand that if he was not expressing his feelings, it was not because he didn't care about what she was saying; he was just overwhelmed. On his part, he needed to make an attempt to speak up more rather than remain intimidated by her.

After I assessed all these communication differences, expressions of feelings and information processing, both husband and wife committed to changing their behaviour to accommodate for each other's approach. They were able to make a positive shift in their relationship and have been living happily since.

Communication Information and details about each colour

The following information provides checklists for you to use to gain a more in-depth understanding of each DISC factor. You will find a checklist that describes the type of work environment that is most ideal for each colour profile, along with the communication tips you will need for interacting with each style.

Ideal Environment for Red
- ☐ Freedom from controls, supervision and details
- ☐ Evaluation based on results, not process or method
- ☐ An innovative, futuristic-oriented environment
- ☐ Non-routine work with challenge and opportunity
- ☐ A forum for them to express their ideas and viewpoints

Communicating with Red
- ☑ Be clear, specific and to the point. Don't ramble on or waste their time
- ☑ Stick to business. Don't try to build personal relationships or chitchat
- ☑ Come prepared with all requirements, objectives and support material in a well-organized package. Don't forget or lose things, be unprepared, disorganized or messy
- ☑ Present the facts logically; plan your presentation efficiently. Don't leave loopholes

- ☑ Ask specific questions. Don't ask rhetorical or useless questions
- ☑ Provide alternatives and choices for making their decisions. Don't come with the decision already made, or make it for them
- ☑ Provide facts and figures about probability of success or the effectiveness of options.

Ideal Environment for Yellow
- ☐ Assignments with a high degree of people contacts
- ☐ Tasks involving motivating groups and establishing a network of contacts
- ☐ Democratic supervisor with whom they can associate
- ☐ Freedom from control and detail
- ☐ Multi-changing work tasks

Communicating with Yellow
- ☑ Allow time for relating and socializing. Don't be curt, cold or tight-lipped. Don't be too businesslike.
- ☑ Talk about people and their goals. Don't go to facts, figures and alternatives.
- ☑ Focus on people and action items. Put details in writing. Don't leave decisions in the air.
- ☑ Ask for their opinion. Don't be impersonal or task-oriented.
- ☑ Provide ideas for implementing action.
- ☑ Provide testimonials from people they see as important or prominent. Don't talk down.

Ideal Environment for Green
- ☐ Jobs for which standards and methods are established
- ☐ Environment where long-standing relationships can be, or are developed

- ☐ Personal attention and appreciation for tasks completed and well done
- ☐ Recognition for loyalty and service
- ☐ Stable and predictable environment
- ☐ Environment where people can be dealt with on a personal, intimate basis

Communicating with Green
- ☑ Start with personal comments. Break the ice. Don't rush headlong into the agenda.
- ☑ Show sincere interest in them as people. Don't stick coldly to business.
- ☑ Patiently draw out their personal goals and ideas. Listen and be responsive.
- ☑ Present your case logically and softly.
- ☑ Ask specific (preferably "How") questions.
- ☑ Move casually, informally. Don't be abrupt.
- ☑ If the situation impacts them personally, look for hurt feelings. Don't mistake their willingness to go along for satisfaction.
- ☑ Provide personal assurances and guarantees. Don't promise something you can't deliver
- ☑ If a decision is required, allow them time to think. Don't force a quick decision.

Ideal Environment for Blue
- ☐ Where critical thinking is needed and rewarded
- ☐ Assignments can be followed through to completion
- ☐ Technical, task-oriented work, specialized area
- ☐ Noise and people are at a minimum
- ☐ Close relationship with small group of people
- ☐ Environment where quality and standards are important

Communicating with Blue

- ☑ Prepare your case in advance. Don't be disorganized or messy.
- ☑ Approach them in a straightforward, direct way. Don't be casual, informal, personal.
- ☑ Build credibility. Don't force a quick decision.
- ☑ Present specifics, and do what you say you can do. Don't be vague about expectations or fail to follow through.
- ☑ Draw up an Action Plan with scheduled dates and milestones. Be conservative.
- ☑ Take your time, but be persistent. Don't be abrupt.
- ☑ If you disagree, prove it with data and facts/testimonials from respected people. Don't appeal to opinions or feelings as evidence.
- ☑ Provide them with the information and time they need to make a decision. Don't use closes – use incentives instead to get the decision.
- ☑ Allow them their space. Don't touch them.

Predicting the Behaviour of Others

In everyday relationships you will meet individuals with their own characteristic way of communicating and interacting with others. Your communication effectiveness, in large, is a measure of your ability to flex to the person you are meeting. In the previous chapter you gained a solid understanding of your own style of communicating. Are you a Red, Yellow, Green or Blue? You have also learned about the DISC framework, which you can use to predict the behaviour of others. Now, let us put it all into practice.

The DISC Communication System is not a personality test. It is a measure of *how* you act. It is about looking at the observable behaviour and emotions of the people around you so that you can predict their colour. This makes this system very valuable, and as you learn to read others you can modify your approach to best suit theirs.

You have just walked into a room full of strangers. You introduce yourself to someone and shake hands. What method will you use to figure out their dominant factor and their colour? You will need to have a system to quickly and efficiently guess their style in 2 minutes or less, so you can begin flexing your behaviour immediately.

For years, I have used the simple method I will now describe. At first, you will have to really pay attention and focus on various details. As this process becomes more automatic, you will develop an unconscious competence. This method for predicting someone's colour involves asking yourself a couple of simple questions:

1. Is the person extroverted or introverted? If the person is an extrovert, you have a Red or Yellow. If the person is an introvert, you have a Blue or Green.
2. Is the person task-oriented or people-oriented? If the person is task-oriented, you have a Red or Blue. If the person is people-oriented, you have a Yellow or a Green.
3. Memorize the chart below to determine the exact colour:

Blue	**Red**
Introverted & Task-oriented	Extroverted & Task-oriented
Green	**Yellow**
Introverted & People-oriented	Extroverted & People-oriented

Your next question should be, *How do you tell the difference between extroverted versus introverted and task-oriented versus people-oriented?* Many of you instinctively know how to distinguish between these characteristics. Follow your instinct. I have worked with so many people who already subconsciously knew how to read people, but were unaware of how they did it so they could not repeat it on command. The DISC framework and many of the techniques you are learning in this book are all designed to provide you with a systematic way of reading behaviour, categorizing it, and then flexing to accommodate the person's style.

After you have made your best guess as to a person's colour, go ahead and flex your behaviour to their style. Remember to treat this like a mini experiment the first few times you try using the method, because you may not get the exact result you expect. As you adjust your behaviour to match someone else's style, you will notice whether or not the person responds differently. If you feel that you are not getting through, try your other best guess and so on. The more you practice using the framework and flexing your behaviour, the more you will master this process.

It is important to point out that the DISC Communication model is a *generalization* of potential behaviour. Every person is unique and so they will not match the characteristics of a colour exactly, but the system does give you a better process for recognizing and categorizing behaviour. This in turn provides a means for us to improve our interactions with others, because we can accommodate for how they communicate, process and take in information.

I have been asked if using a system like this makes us appear to not be genuine. My response is that if we have an opportunity to be a better listener or to shift our response to better get through to the person with whom we are communicating, then these techniques are serving a valuable purpose and is an expression of our keen desire to build more effective relationships. If you are sincere in the application of these tools, the other person can only appreciate that you have gone to the trouble of learning to communicate the way they need.

Recognizing the Colours based on Body Language and Tonality

In addition to the techniques discussed above, you can also predict an individual's DISC colour using the following chart. It displays each colour group's specific body language, tone and words that they have a tendency to express. Start by memorizing a few points from each section for each colour. Then put it all into practice by reading people you meet around the office. The more you connect the information in the chart to a real person, the more it will stick in your mind.

	Body Language	Tone of Voice	Pace / Speech	Words / Content
Red	Keep your distance Strong handshake Direct eye contact Controlled gestures Lean forward	Strong Clear, loud Confident Direct	Fast / Abrupt	Win, Lead the field, Results, Now, New, Challenge

Yellow	Get close Use touch Relaxed, humor Friendly eye contact Expressive gestures	Enthusiastic High and low modulation Friendly Energized	Fast / Skip around	Fun, I feel, Sociable, Will make you look good, Exciting
Green	Relaxed Methodical Lean back Friendly eye contact Small gestures	Warm Soft Steady Low volume	Leisurely / Logical	Step-by-step Help me out Guarantee Promise Think about it
Blue	Keep your distance Firm posture Direct eye contact No gestures	Controlled Direct Thoughtful Little modulation	Precise / Logical	Here are the facts No risk Proven Analysis Guarantees

Adapted from The Universal Language DISC B. Bonnstetter, et al.

CHAPTER SEVEN

Team Building with the Colours

Now that you have a clear understanding of the DISC Communication Model, we can look at how it can be used to assist in team building. A typical team is made up of a variety of colours. A study by TTI breaks down the North American population into the following colour groups:

- Red = 18%
- Yellow = 28%
- Green = 40%
- Blue = 14%

We will encounter each and every style in our workplace and home. You will also find that these demographics shift depending on the type of business. There will usually be more Blues in engineering companies, more Reds and Yellows in sales-oriented companies, more Yellows and Greens in human services companies and health care. As discussed, the way you can communicate effectively with each of these colours is by adapting your own style to theirs.

You can imagine how many clashes between colours occur due to a perceived incompatibility in how team members complete tasks and behave in interpersonal situations. Time and time again, I have been brought in to work with companies that complained of staff conflict and lost productivity, only to discover that often at the crux of things lay a fundamental difference in communication styles.

I have utilized the DISC model in my work with thousands of teams and individuals over the past 20 years. One of the key steps we complete as part of a team building program is to identify each team member's colour through an online validated profiling system. We usually take the time to review each person's unique value to the team, their communication approach to tasks and interpersonal relationships, and the motivational elements they require to perform at their maximum potential.

We then facilitate a variety of exercises and scenarios where employees engage with each other using this new knowledge of their coworkers and teammates to enhance their working relationship. I have found that instead of expending energy in disagreement, the teams I've worked with have permanently improved their interactions. Their dramatic improvement stems from the fact that they now have the tools and framework to actively demonstrate behavioural flexibility with each other.

In addition to working with private corporations, I also work with not-for-profit organizations that are looking to enhance their team effectiveness. I'll never forget one situation that occurred in a community-based agency, where team members were having a very difficult time organizing themselves to get the work done. Each member had a different approach. Everyone was bickering and blaming others for failing to share the workload. I was brought in to assist this dysfunctional team.

In the first step of the process, which I call Discovery, I simply observed team members in their workplace. They were required to plan and work through a list of activities to assist individuals living in a group home setting. Typically, two individuals would work together on a shift, and support each other through a work cycle. I noticed that one staff member (let's call her Mary), immediately upon arrival for her shift, began creating a list of to-dos, and without even saying hello to her colleague she began to work through the list. The other staff member (who we'll call Jane) tried to connect with Mary with a friendly hello as soon as she arrived. Mary gave her a furtive glance and said only, "We've got lots to do" before carrying on with her tasks. Jane grimaced and was clearly hurt by Mary's abruptness, whereas Mary appeared oblivious.

Based upon my observations, I assessed that Mary was a Red task-oriented person and Jane was a Green people-oriented person. No wonder they weren't getting along – here we had the extremes on the spectrum in terms of work focus and conversational style. In my interview with Mary, she said that Jane always wanted to chit-chat and waste time, and she was fed up of tying to get her to work faster. Mary herself was not interested in talking about the weather and personal stuff. She was paid to work, not to socialize.

In my interview with Jane, she accused Mary of being unfriendly and always in a rush. All Mary wanted was to boss her around and be pushy, having an attitude of "Hurry up and work faster and stop trying to be my friend." Jane said that she felt hurt but did not want to speak up and cause more conflict with Mary. She felt that Mary misunderstood her attempts at wanting the day to go by in a more relaxed way, as an attempt to socialize all day and distract Mary from her work.

I got each individual to complete an online profile that provided them with a detailed report of their DISC assessment. We worked together to so they could learn about each other's approach to work and communication. Mary was counseled to give a simple greeting to her co-workers when she arrived on a shift, and to share the responsibility of creating the task list. She recognized that her sense of urgency was not necessarily reasonable, and that her need for achievement often caused her to be impatient with others. She further acknowledged that she was definitely pushing Jane to meet an unrealistic standard.

Jane was counseled to speak up and participate in the creation of task lists, and to quickly get to the point when addressing Mary. She recognized that she was stubbornly slowing things down at times because Mary was unfriendly to her. She acknowledged that Mary had good intentions in trying to get things done, and it was not a personal attack when she was being abrupt. But Jane wanted to maintain her friendly approach. Often they finished their work early, so she explained to Mary her objective of wanting to have a more relaxed environment and not feel so stressed at work.

This situation may seem like déjà vu to you, because by this point in your career you probably have felt that you were one of these two people. Were you Mary or were you Jane? The challenge I had was being able to help Mary and Jane see that both their approaches to work were equally valid. It was obvious that they were both judging each other, feeling that their own personal approach was the best. This was a clear stand-off, with either worker feeling they were right and their colleague was wrong. It took a few coaching sessions with each individual to recognize where they had inherited their work ethic and why they were viewing their coworker so harshly.

Mary was the oldest of all her siblings in a family with four children. Her parents both worked and were very busy throughout the week, so she often had the duty of taking care of her siblings. She alone had to organize their dinners and the clean-up. Because she would not have any free time until her sisters and brother got everything that needed to get done, she learned to prioritize and delegate tasks very effectively. Mary would look forward to the few hours of free time she dedicated to doing things she wanted to do. She remembered how wonderful she felt when her parents would praise her on how organized she was and what a great job she did managing her siblings. We can see that Mary was repeatedly rewarded for her task efficiency, which reinforced her approach to work as an adult.

Jane, the youngest of two children, felt that she had to compete with her older brother for her parents' affection. She became the friendly and fun child who would talk with her parents about all the things she did at school and about how she got along so well with her peers. She remembered how great it felt when her teacher gave her a prize for being the most helpful student in class, which made her parents very proud. Jane felt that being friendly and kind were among the most important values in a person. Here we see that Jane was rewarded for her people skills, which reinforced her approach to work as an adult.

This classic example illustrates how a conflict between task and people orientation can affect team work. If you are a Red or Blue, the next time you enter the office of a Green or Yellow take a moment to say hello and find out how your coworker's day is going. Alternatively, if you are a Green or Yellow and you enter the office of a Red or Blue, after a quick hello then don't be shy to jump right into the business discussion. All parties will feel that you have taken the time to understand what they need in the communication process.

Even though we all have a strong preference or intensity toward one of the specific DISC factors, in actuality we possess all the factors in our profile, to varying levels. Whenever I work with teams, I help them to recognize that all the colours are equal and each of the DISC styles brings an important value to the team. Recognize that Reds will drive the process toward the result; Yellows will generate ideas and solutions; Blues will drill down to the detailed planning and then develop the policies, procedures and systems; and finally, Greens will stick though the implementation and support the team.

The following tables provide a summary of the Communication Dos and Don'ts for each colour, as well as the value they bring to the organization and the possible limitations of each. Team members should use these charts to understand each other's dominant approach, the flex to each other.

Red – High Dominance Factor
When communicating with a person who is ambitious, forceful, decisive, strong-willed, risk-taking, independent and goal-oriented:

Communication Do's	Communication Don'ts
1. Be clear, specific, brief and to the point 2. Stick to business 3. Be prepared with support material in a well-organized "package"	Factors that create tension or dissatisfaction: 1. Talking about things that are not relevant to the issue 2. Leaving loopholes or cloudy issues 3. Appearing disorganized

The Value of Red to the Team	Possible Limitations of Red:
1. Bottom-line organizer 2. Self-starter 3. Forward-looking 4. Places high value on time 5. Challenge-oriented 6. Competitive 7. Initiates activity 8. Challenges the status quo 9. Innovative and Tenacious	• Oversteps authority • Too directive • Impatient with others • Takes on too many tasks and focuses too heavily on tasks

Yellow – High Influence Factor

When communicating with a person who is magnetic, enthusiastic, friendly, and demonstrative:

Communication Do's	Communication Don'ts
1. Provide a warm and friendly environment 2. Don't deal with a lot of details (put them in writing) 3. Ask "feeling" questions to draw their opinions or comments	Factors that create tension or dissatisfaction: 1. Being curt, cold or tight-lipped 2. Controlling the conversation 3. Driving on facts and figures, alternatives, abstractions
The Value of Yellow to the Team 1. Optimism and enthusiasm 2. Creative problem-solving 3. Motivates others toward goals 4. Positive sense of humour 5. Team player 6. Negotiates conflict 7. Verbalizes articulately	**Possible Limitations of Yellow:** • Oversells and is impulsive; heart over mind • Trusts people indiscriminately • Is inattentive to detail • Overestimates ability to motivate others or change behaviour

	• Under-instructs and over-delegates • Overuses hand motions and facial expressions while talking

Green- High Steadiness Factor

When communicating with a person who is patient, predictable, reliable, steady, relaxed and supportive:

Communication Do's	Communication Don'ts
1. Begin with a personal comment – break the ice 2. Present your case softly, non-threatening 3. Ask "how?" questions to draw their opinions	Factors that create tension or dissatisfaction: 1. Rushing headlong into business 2. Being domineering or demanding 3. Forcing them to respond quickly to your objectives
The Value of Green to the Team 1. Dependable team worker 2. Works hard for a leader and a cause 3. Great listener 4. Patient and empathetic 5. Good at reconciling factions, calming and stabilizing 6. Logical and step-wise thinker 7. Will finish tasks started 8. Loyal, long-term relationships	**Possible Limitations of Green:** • Takes criticism of work as a personal insult • Resists change just for the sake of it • Has difficulty establishing priorities • Internalizes feelings when they should actually be discussed • Gives a false sense of compliance • Too hard on themselves • May stay involved in a situation too long

Blue- High Compliance Factor

When communicating with a person who is serious, conservative, perfectionist, cautious and compliant:

Communication Do's	Communication Don'ts
1. Prepare your case in advance 2. Stick to business 3. Be accurate and realistic	Factors that create tension or dissatisfaction: 1. Being giddy, casual, informal, loud 2. Pushing too hard or being unrealistic with deadlines 3. Being disorganized or messy
The Value of Blue to the Team 1. Objective thinker 2. Conscientious about procedures 3. Perfectionist. Maintains high standards 4. Precise and attentive to small details 5. Defines, clarifies, gets information, criticizes and tests 6. Task-oriented 7. Asks the right questions 8. Diplomatic 9. By-the-book; needs proof and evidence	**Possible Limitations of Blue:** • Hesitates to act without precedent • Overanalyzes: Analysis Paralysis • Too critical of others • Gets bogged down in details • Doesn't verbalize feelings, but internalizes them • Defensive when criticized • Yields position to avoid controversy • Too hard on themselves

CHAPTER EIGHT

Learning styles (Representational Systems)

I remember being in fourth grade and wondering why the teacher did not allow us to talk about what we were learning, show us pictures or write more notes on the board. Back then I was not aware that I was not only an external processor, but I also needed to *see* what she was talking about. As a visual learner, it was essential for me to see images and written notes in order to fully grasp the lesson.

The field of psychology and studies of the mind has advanced exponentially since then. It is now recognized that the ways we perceive and process information are uniquely-tailored to each individual. We encode information differently based upon our senses, and there is a solid body of research that describes visual, auditory and kinaesthetic learning styles. The good news is that many educational institutions are now incorporating differentiated teaching practices to take into account the diverse ways students learn and communicate.

When we conjure up a memory or think about an earlier experience, our minds produce a representation of that memory. One simple trick for figuring out your dominant learning style is to think back to your last birthday party. Do you remember the colour (visual) or texture (tactile) of wrapping on the gift boxes? Does the memory appear as a picture, or do you repeat a story about the event? Do you recall what it felt like when your guests sang to you? Do you taste the chocolate cake or smell the coffee you drank with it? Our subjective reality is replayed in our mind through the sensory cues we associate with the experience we had.

Communication starts with from our beliefs, which in turn produce our thoughts. We use words, vocal cues and body language to convey these thoughts. In a nutshell, thoughts are experienced as internal representations of what our five senses perceive. We re-experience life based on the sensory information we initially perceived, such as feelings, sights, and sounds.

Think about how you remember. Do you see pictures, hear sounds, relive the feelings, or do you re-experience tastes and smells? A constant barrier to communication is that we often assume other people think the same way we do, and so we present information the way we would want it presented to us, rather than how someone else needs it.

As a developer and facilitator of numerous presentations and courses, I recognize the importance of writing for multiple types of audiences. In all my workshops I make sure to employ a combination of several multi-sensory instructional approaches in order to ensure that each learner is engaged. These multi-sensory techniques activate and stimulate our brains on multiple channels. We are seeing, hearing and feeling simultaneously, enhancing the experience and making the information more impactful.

Various studies have supported the importance of learning styles. In a 1993 study by Sandra Rief, who is renowned for her research with students with ADHD, she found that students retain information in the following manner:

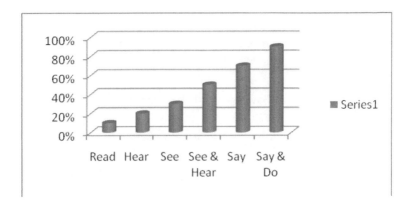

- 10% remember what they read
- 20% remember what they hear
- 30% what they see
- 50% what they see and hear
- 70% what they say
- 90% what they say and do

Our learning style is defined by the preference for a particular sense that is utilized as our dominant way of focusing, processing, encoding, retain and retrieving information or stimuli.

One of the most prevalent models for multiplying learning styles was developed by Neil Fleming in 1987. This learning model was given the acronym **VARK** for **Visual, Aural, Read/write and Kinesthetic**. Fleming theory described these learning styles as indicative of people's subconscious preference for one of the four styles. In practice, when information is presented in the person's preferred style, they perform better at the learning task. Fleming felt that we are predisposed to instinctively favour one style versus another.

Visual learners want information presented to them so that they can see it; **Aural learners** (also called

Auditory) want to hear and listen; **Kinesthetic learners** (also called tactile) want to experience the learning, and **Read/write learners** want to read and then re-write in order to learn.

Fleming's model was an expansion of the VAK learning model, which was described in **Neuro-Linguistic Programming (NLP)** in the mid-seventies. NLP is a body of knowledge that was co-founded by Richard Bandler (a student at the University of California) and John Grinder (a linguist at the same university). The term was coined to describe the foundational belief of the model that there are connections between neurological and linguistic processes which form specific behavioural patterns that have been programmed in us based upon our life experiences.

Such patterns would be elicited to determine their effectiveness, and through NLP tools one could change their mental, emotional and physical behaviour. Neuro-linguistic programming, now also called neuro-linguistic psychology, is being put into use today in many sectors including leadership/management development, sports, therapeutic counseling, and life coaching. Practitioners of NLP utilize the tools to develop the capacity to challenge the distortions, generalizations and deletions expressed through their clients' language. Many of the behavioural modification and counseling techniques I have utilized in my own practice stem from NLP foundations: specifically, NLP practices that include anchoring, reframing, and rapport building. These and other references to NLP are discussed throughout this book.

In NLP, the learning model is described as our **representational system**s, while in other literature you may encounter it under the term *sensory modalities*. The representational system defines how our minds process information through the use of our senses. The model's

acronym is **VAKOG**, which refers to **visual, auditory, kinesthetic, olfactory and gustatory**. Specifically, it is said that:
- visual people see, then create pictures in their heads;
- auditory people hear, then talk to themselves;
- kinesthetic people feel, then evaluate these feelings through their bodies;
- olfactory people smell, then process the scents; and
- gustatory people taste, then process the tastes.

Filtered through our perceptions, we represent sensory realities in our minds in different ways, which become how we store our experiences and memories. You have probably experienced a situation where you find yourself mentally rehearsing for something by talking to yourself, or mentally visualizing by creating imagery in your mind. Although we constantly use all our senses, as with the DISC communication system, we have a dominant representation system (which I may also refer to as your learning style), that is situation-specific.

Among the four sensory modalities, we are more likely to rely on our visual, auditory or kinesthetic senses, with one of these taking the lead in how we encode the stimuli we receive. We will now review each of the VAK modalities.

Visual Representational System

We can describe visual learners, or those with a visual representational system, as people who think in terms of images and pictures. During a presentation you will see visual learners taking notes, especially if the presenter makes notes on the whiteboard. Visual learners prefer to have a handout of any text-based materials. To effectively encode material for a visual learner, it is best to use illustrations, maps, graphs, charts and other visual media to represent the information you are conveying. They remember best by *seeing the learning*.

How do you recognize if your dominant representation system is visual? Picture yourself sitting in a lecture – do you find yourself wanting to draw or doodle? Do you find it easier to read the materials and make your own notes, rather than listen to the person speaking? Visual learners typically have a great sense of direction and will engage more with content that is in colour. They give themselves away by using words related to seeing such as:
- I *see* what you are saying
- Can we *look* at this more closely?
- I have a different *perspective* on this
- Can you *picture* what I am trying to *illustrate*?

Always remember that when you communicate with someone with a visual representation system, it's important to use visual aids and visual language so they can see what you are telling them. For example: you're about to review a proposal with a new prospect, who you have determined primarily takes in information visually. Your proposal should summarize information in word webs, tables, charts and diagrams. Also aim to use a mind map to depict the main points of the proposal so he/she can glance at the content. You should meet in a place where you will not have visual distractions; that is, try to avoid meeting on a restaurant patio where there are televisions all around, waiters buzzing around, lots of people coming and going. When you are having a conversation with a visual, you should use visual key words for such as *see, picture* and *vision*.

I usually provide a notepad, pen and highlighter, and wherever possible I encourage the visual person to write down or highlight key information. As a visual learner myself, I remember my own techniques of writing down crib sheets whenever I wanted to memorize things when I studied.

You will want to avoid giving only verbal instructions to those with a visual representation system. Can you think of someone who you believe is a visual learner? Do they seem to make more mistakes when you tell them instructions face-to-face versus when you send them an email? It is possible that you are providing only oral information and the person wants to *see* what you are saying!

Auditory Representational System

Auditory learners or those whose dominant representational system is auditory prefer to listen to your message. They're the individuals who you'll see intently watching the lips of the lecturer. They want to have group discussions, read out loud and lectures when learning. Auditory learners can be seen sub-vocalizing (repeating silently to themselves), or repeating out loud what they have heard. They will use words and language as they primary form of communicating with others. They are very distracted by noise. I have a good friend who will often squeeze her hands over her ears whenever she is trying to think, or turn her head sideways to expose her stronger ear when she is actively listening to someone. These are both very strong signs of an auditory learner.

You can figure out if your dominant representation system is auditory if you find that you prefer to read written information out loud to yourself. Think about what you do when you review an email. Do you find yourself repeating key phrases of the message to really understand or remember them? Realize that verbal repetition and

recall is the best method for you to learn. They give themselves away by using words related to seeing such as:
- I *hear* you
- That *sounds* like a great idea
- *Tell* me what you want

Communication effectiveness can be increased with an auditory learner by facing them directly when you are speaking. Emphasize core elements of the message by verbally repeating these components, and have the person say aloud the information by asking them to paraphrase. Auditory learners do need the time to vocalize the message to themselves in order to fully process the meaning, so leave time for them to do this. If it is appropriate, you can associate special sounds or music to the information you want them to remember. Using auditory key words such as hear and sound will stimulate the listener to pay attention more acutely.

I always pair oral and written information when I provide materials to those with an auditory representation system, also ensuring that there is sufficient time for discussion and problem-solving in groups. I frequently use podcasts or video clips, as well as give time for private reflection or reading during my workshops so that auditory learners have a chance to review the content on their own. In addition, I include question and answer periods throughout so that the auditory person can talk it through to make the learning make sense to them.

Kinesthetic Representational System

Tactile or kinesthetic learners learn by doing. They want to touch, feel and experience the learning process, and prefer to write things down while listening in order to jot their memory later. You will notice tactile learners frequently holding an object in their hand; they'll often pick up an object such as a water bottle or pen when you are speaking to them. The physical sensation of the object in their hand helps them to *grasp* what you are saying. As a sidebar, these individuals can be great at physical activities like sports.

You are a tactile learner if you prefer to learn by doing hands-on training. You respond well to information that is provided in a step-by-step format that describes how to do things. You typically find it hard to sit still for long periods of time, instead preferring to pace back and forth, or fidget by tapping fingers and toes. If you are standing, you may shift your weight from one leg to the other; if sitting, you might shake your legs or squeeze your fists when listening. Kinesthetic learners give themselves away by using words related to seeing such as:

- I *feel* / I understand
- That is a *solid* idea
- I have a good *grasp* of what you're telling me

When I work with kinesthetic learners, I make sure to get them doing what they are learning. Workshops are designed to include many experiential components that provide opportunities for role playing, hands-on simulations and active manipulation of the environment. Communication is enhanced with tactile learners when there are a variety of different activities they can engage in during a lecture, in addition to periodic stretch breaks. Completion of real-life tasks, trips, surveys and experimentation are all important learning aids for those with the kinesthetic representational system.

Communicating with the tactile person requires that you discuss things step-by-step, as if you were physically walking through the information, and then give them the chance to write while you are speaking. They need processing time to *feel* that they understand you. Remember to use physical key words such as *feel, hear,* and *grip* when speaking with a kinesthetic learner.

Auditory-Digital Representational System

Recently in NLP they have been describing a new, emerging learning style called Auditory-Digital. These individuals have a preference for dialogue that is presented in a logical and sequential manner. Unlike the other learning styles, this style is not related to one of the five sensory inputs. These learners encode their experiences in abstract constructs that they retrieve by sometimes closing their eyes or looking away from the speaker. They are also prone to sub-vocalizing when they are learning or thinking things through, so don't be surprised if you see them talking to themselves.

There is a belief that our world of virtual experiences and digital, online interactions are contributing to the evolution of this learning style. Auditory Digital learners can be distracted by illogical arguments, which are difficult for them to process in an abstract manner. They also tend to use these expressions:
- I *understand*
- that makes *sense* to me

Take this Quick Learning Style Assessment

1. *I can remember what I am learning if I take the time to talk about it, rather than just reading about it.* If you answered yes to this statement, you are an auditory learner.
2. *I can remember what I am learning if I see pictures, images and get to write about it.* If you answered yes to this statement, you are a visual learner.

> 3. *I can remember what I am learning if I get to work with my hands or get involved in demonstrations of the materials.* If you answered yes to this statement, you are a kinesthetic learner.
> 4. *I can remember what I am learning if I can repeat the words quietly to myself and work it out logically in my mind.* If you answered yes to this statement, you are an auditory-digital learner.

The Prescription: Recognizing Learning Styles

So far this chapter has provided a description of learning styles, how to figure out your own style, and how to communicate more effectively with each of the other styles. You might have already figured out that this book was constructed with these principles in mind. There are words, pictures, charts, tables and hands-on exercises to engage and appeal to each style.

The following table provides a snapshot of the chapter highlights, and can be used to quickly recognize a person's representational system.

Item	Visual	Auditory	Kinesthetic	Auditory Digital
Words used	See, picture, perspective	Hear, listen, sounds	Feel, solid, grasp, grounded	Sense, under-stand
Common phrases	I see what you mean	I hear you	I feel I understand you	It makes sense to me
Breathing pattern	High in the chest or throat	Middle part of the chest	Lower abdomen	Middle part of the chest

Speed of speech	Fastest speakers Words have to keep up with the pictures	Moderate rate of speech	Slowest speakers	Moderate rate of speech
Distractions	Movement Flashing images	Noise Words in music	Environmental Heat, Cold Vibration	Illogical arguments
Communication tips	Show them! Use their words & phrases	Tell them! Say it out loud Use their words & phrases	Let them do it! Use their words & phrases	Let them repeat it! Use their words & phrases
Learning Aids	Images, graphs, charts, diagrams, mind maps	Words, discussion videos w/ text	Role-play, simulations, demonstrations	Logical concept development, Logical steps

We can take advantage of our knowledge of learner styles because we understand how people internally code their experiences. Whether via written or verbal communication, we can connect on a subconscious basis with others by modifying our language and behaviour to reflect their specific representational system. We must speak their language, i.e. we have to use the precise words for auditory, kinesthetic, visual or auditory digital.

As you recognize someone's learning preference, you need to then begin to express your message predominantly in a way that relates specifically to their preferred sensory modality. Essentially, you will be tailoring and matching the other person's words and phrases to better create understanding, which will lead to tangible results and significant improvement in communication.

Take a second right now to think about some of the people around you – your significant other, your boss or a good friend. Compare what you know about them to the chart above.

What is their learning style?

What are their tell-tale signs?

Write down one thing you will do differently the next time you communicate with them:

Favoured Representational System Recap

Representational systems are the way you take in information, perceive and code memories. There are four major representational systems: Visual, Auditory, Kinesthetic and Auditory Digital. Two other representational systems are Olfactory and Gustatory. Our preferred representational system affects what we see, hear, feel, our breathing, our body posture and the way we move our eyes.

V: Visual
People who are visual often stand or sit with their heads and/or bodies erect. They will breathe from the top of their lungs. They often sit forward in their chair, memorize by seeing pictures, and are less distracted by noise. They often have trouble remembering verbal instructions because their minds tend to

wander. A visual person will be interested in how your program LOOKS. Appearances are important to them.

A: Auditory
People who are auditory will move their eyes sideways. They breathe from the middle of their chest. They typically talk to themselves (sub-vocalize), and are easily distracted by noise. They can repeat things back to you easily, they learn by listening, and usually like music and talking on the phone. They memorize by steps, procedures, and sequences (sequentially). The auditory person likes to be TOLD how they're doing, and responds to a certain tone of voice or set of words. They will be interested in what you have to say about your program.

K: Kinesthetic
People who are kinesthetic will typically be breathing from the bottom of their lungs, so you'll see their stomach go in and out when they breathe. They often walk and talk slower than other styles. They memorize by doing or walking through something. They will be interested in your program if it "feels right".

Ad: Auditory Digital
These persons may spend a fair amount of time talking to themselves. Logic plays a key role in their decision process, as do facts and figures. The auditory digital person can exhibit characteristics of the other major representational systems.

CHAPTER NINE

Building Subconscious Rapport

Several years ago I stopped at a coffee shop for afternoon tea. As I sat enjoying my beverage, I overheard a woman also ordering a tea. "Earl Grey, please," she said. The reason I noticed her was that I had just ordered my tea using those exact three words, which seemed coincidental. I looked over at the woman and noticed that she had a book under her arm with the word "Mentoring" on the title.

This was also significant because I had recently started a company called Technology Mentors that offered web development and system solutions consulting. One of the key services we provided was Y2K remediation, which at the time was in great demand. (This becomes important later in the conversation we are about to have).

A minute later, the woman took the table closest to mine. Once she was settled in her seat, I turned to her and said, "Hi, I couldn't help noticing you ordered an Earl Grey, my favourite tea – is it yours too?" "Yes," she said. "I really enjoy it." I turned and offered her my business card, then made reference to the fact that the book she was reading had the word mentoring, a key word in my company name. "Oh, this is interesting, tell me about what you do," she said.

I told her all about our concept, which included the recruitment and mentoring of new information technology graduates by senior IT consultants. We would place these new fledging consultants into organizations with a seasoned project manager to work on various technology projects. This also meant cost savings for an organization since they would not be hiring only high-priced talent. We wanted to bridge the gap between the technical and business units as well.

She expressed that she really believed in this approach and was literally just sitting at the coffee shop wondering how she might find a consultant who could work with her to develop methodologies for managing the many IT projects her company was embarking on. As it turned out, she was the CEO of a financial management company who needed Y2K remediation assistance and a number of the key services that my company was offering.

In addition to these coincidences, our conversation was very interesting in other ways, due to the many synergies we found between ourselves. Periodically, she would use the word "absolutely", and I found myself naturally using the same word throughout our chat. The conversation was fast-paced, direct, and we both scribbled down key words and facts on a handy notepad which we both pulled out of our bags simultaneously. I often would draw little circles creating a mind map to display what I talking about, while she would begin to add her own circles to the schematic. Our time together lasted a couple of hours, by the end of which we had decided that we would work together.

This CEO not only hired me for her company, but also introduced me to a number of her colleagues who later became clients. This single coffee shop meeting resulted in several hundred thousand dollars worth of business for my company.

I have shared this story with you to impress upon you the importance of **rapport building**. The conversation with the woman in the coffee shop included several elements of subconscious rapport building. We liked the same tea; we used many of the same words; we both liked making pictures of our ideas; we had similar gestures; we did things simultaneously; and we had common interests. We were alike in many ways, which facilitated subconscious trust between us.

I believe that establishing and maintaining rapport with someone is the foundation of effective communication. Rapport establishes trust which builds relationships. When I am asked to define rapport, I will usually say that *"when people are like each other, they tend to like each other."*

Realize that our subconscious provides constant surveillance of our environment, looking for what is *different*. Different means unpredictable, and therefore our subconscious will interpret different as unsafe. However, if we see something familiar, our subconscious will relax. This is part of the underlying psychology that makes rapport building work. If I can make you feel at ease and that we are alike, you will trust me. With this trust we can have great communication and develop a deeper connection.

Rapport is the feeling of being in *sync* with each other. People who have expressed how they feel when they are in rapport with another will say things like:
- I felt that I knew the person longer than I really did
- We seemed to be able to complete each other's sentences
- It was as if they were reading my mind
- They asked if we had met before

You can observe people naturally forming rapport by watching them at a restaurant or bar. Notice how many among a party of friends lift their glasses or forks at the same time. It is as if there is an invisible symphony conductor orchestrating the whole scene. Rapport creates an environment of trust where everyone feels comfortable expressing themselves freely.

The most successful salespeople in the world use rapport building techniques as an effective tool for quickly building business relationships. In my work with top sales executives, they testify to the power of mirroring client behaviours as an aide to help establish client confidence, which leads to more sales.

Politicians are renounced for using subconscious rapport building techniques or to project a certain public image. A few of years ago I saw a photo of George W. Bush and Tony Blair attending UN meetings over the war on Iraq. It was a very interesting picture because there were so many common elements. They were mirror images of each other. They both had exactly the same expression: their elbows were on the table and their hands on their chin. They wore similar suits, and both had chosen a red tie. There were the same number of water bottles on the table beside each man, with two clear bottles and one green one. Finally, the words United Kingdom and United States were placed strategically on a plaque in front of them. This picture sent an immediate subconscious message that they were indeed a united force.

Another image that illustrates the use of rapport in politics is one I found on the internet with Obama posing in front of a statue of Superman. Obama had adopted the same posture as the man of steel – hands on his hips, the same determined, unwavering facial expression. This was one of the photos taken on his first campaign for the presidency. The message sent by his campaigners was clear: he *was* Superman. It may seem tongue and cheek, but the subliminal messages orchestrated by the presidential publicity campaigns go right into the subconscious mind where the association is already made.

We see the use of rapport in leadership, where we are told to *walk the talk*. It is a well-known fact that people will *do as we do* much more than they will *do as we say*. Great leaders will therefore model behaviour for their teams. They know that in order to have people follow them, they must set the example.

I have seen this work both in a negative and a positive way. Five years ago I was hired to assist with improving an organization's communication and team cohesiveness. The biggest complaint they had was that team members were not very responsive to each other, either through voicemail or email. Upon observing all levels of the organization, I discovered that the company president ignored many of the messages sent to him and his responses were inconsistent.

The first point of intervention was to work with him to increase his responsiveness to the team. At first he was reluctant, citing that he got hundreds of messages and it was not feasible for him to have to deal with them. Everyone else had much fewer messages so they had different expectations. I indicted to him that even if he developed a strategy to respond to each of his direct reports at least once daily based upon the organizational priorities, he would at the very least be developing a new culture of responsiveness.

Within two months he began to shift his behaviour. We created a mechanism for filtering his emails and voicemails, and set aside time in his calendar each day for responding to emails and voicemails. Gradually he saw a shift in the behaviour of team members which enhanced their overall corporate communication.

Rapport Building Techniques

By now you should have a greater appreciation of the importance of rapport in personal relationships, sales, politics and leadership. We will now go over the techniques for building instant subconscious rapport with someone you meet for the first time, or strengthen the rapport you have with someone you already know.

You have learned a number of tools for creating a strong connection with others. When you change your communication to match a person's colour or shift how you present information due to someone's learning style, you are already building rapport. Rapport building involves any change in your behaviour or language that is designed to match or accommodate the other person.

Mirroring and matching the behaviour of the person with whom you are interacting is the most instant way to create rapport. To **mirror** someone's behaviour means that you do exactly what they are doing. If they cross their arms, then you should be crossing your arms; if they cross their legs, do it also. To **match** someone's behaviour means that you are approximating their gestures. Specific ways to build rapport (any of these can be done and not all are required at once) happen by:
- Matching the person's body language
- Matching the person's voice and tone
- Matching the person's breathing
- Matching the person's words and common experiences

In 1990, Italian brain researchers made an amazing discovery about brain cells they are calling mirror neurons. Mirror neurons could well be the foundation of how rapport and empathy works on a neurological level. Researchers wanted to find out how we have the ability to instinctively understand what someone else is experiencing by just observing them. If you see someone stub their toe, you might just find yourself flinching in empathy, as if you stubbed your toe too.

Mirror neurons became the answer — these are a special class of brain cells that fire not only when an individual performs an action, but also when the individual observes someone else make the same movement, assisting us in knowing exactly what the other person is experiencing.

Studies were conducted where subjects observed the same action, such as grasping a cup in different contexts, such as to drink from it or to clean it. This elicited *different levels* of mirror neuron activity in the mirror neuron system. This finding shows that the mirror neuron system does more than code the observed action, i.e. grasping the cup. It also appears to code the intention behind the action (grasping the cup to drink or grasping the cup to clear a table).

Mirror neuron research is helping scientists to interpret the neurological basis of social interactions and provide evidence of the power of building subconscious rapport. You are not just mirroring and matching visible verbal and non-verbal cues, you might just be mirroring on a neurological level as well.

Match Body Language

Matching a person's body language includes paying attention and matching posture, gestures, facial expressions and even the rate of blinking. Are they sitting forward in their chair? You might begin by sitting back, and then gradually sit forward at peak points in the dialogue.

Visuals and Reds tend to sit more erect so you will build rapport with them if you do this too.

What are the person's hands and feet doing? Almost everyone crosses and uncrosses their arms and/or legs at some point in a conversation. A part of your repertoire of gestures should be folding your arms and crossing your legs as well.

A genuine smile is the universal tool for establishing rapport. Guillaume Duchenne, a French anatomist who studied emotional expression through the electrical stimulation of the severed heads of criminals, published his research in a in 1862. His findings indicated that the major muscles in the cheeks can always be forced to create a smile (i.e. a fake smile), but the muscles around the eyes contract during a real smile, which creates what we now call crow's feet. The name Duchenne smile was applied to this type of "genuine smile."

Facial expressions, such as a smile, are a barometer of emotions (Izard, 1971), and like emotions, they vary in form and intensity. Previous studies have found that positive emotions, as inferred from smile intensity in childhood photos and college yearbook photos, are correlated with marriage stability and satisfaction (Harker & Keltner, 2001; Hertenstein et al, 2009).

Emotions affect personalities and life outcomes by influencing how people think, behave, and interact with others (Izard, 1971). People with positive emotions are happier and have more stable personalities, more stable marriages, and better cognitive and interpersonal skills than those with negative emotions, throughout the life span (Harker & Keltner, 2001; Hertenstein et al, 2009).

A more recent study published in the Psychological Science journal is the first to link smile intensity to a biological outcome: longevity. In their 2010 study, Ernest

Abel and Michael Kruger published their research on professional baseball players, rating their smiles to longevity. They compared the smiles of players in their 1952 yearbook, then reviewed how each player aged upon death. They found that players with Duchenne smiles in their yearbook photo were statistically shown to live longer.

Not only will a smile enhance your well-being, but the next time you really want to create an instant deep emotional connection with someone, flash them a genuine smile.

Match Tonality

Next, pay close attention to how the person is speaking. We want to work on matching the person's tone of voice, their speed of speech and the volume they are speaking. Are they talking quickly or slowly? Recall how we discussed that visuals speak quicker than kinesthetic learners, who tend to speak the slowest. Adjust your speed of speech to match the person with whom you are talking.

Are they speaking loudly or softly? Greens tend to speak the softest among all the colours. Does the person have a low deep voice or a higher pitched voice? If you speak quickly, you need to practice slowing down your speech and possibly speaking quieter than usual so that you match a slower speaker and vice versa.

Matching someone's tonality (volume, speed and pitch), is the best method to build rapport with someone over the phone or through virtual online meetings.

Match Words and Common Experiences

You should remember from my coffee shop experience that matching someone's **key words and phrases** can truly help in building rapport. We usually don't listen closely enough to notice a person's favoured discrete words or phrases. Our mind focuses on full sentences to comprehend the message; to determine context and to pick up on the emotional content.

In order to mirror and match a person's words during a conversation, you need to listen for words or expressions that are used often or repeated periodically. You might also notice patterns in the phrasing that the other person is using. Such words and phrasing are tools that can serve an important purpose in subconscious influence; as such, you must sharpen your listening skills in order to catch things that you can put to good use later in the conversation.

Common experiences can be created by discussing subject areas that each person has specific knowledgeable about. Hobbies or common interests (i.e. golfing, cooking, games, music, dance, and travel) can become the basis for building verbal rapport. When we are very comfortable with a subject, we find it easy to just relax and share our interests and passions with others.

Match breathing where appropriate

Breathing patterns vary among people. Think about someone you know very well. Have you ever paid attention to how this person breathes? What is the pace of their breathing? Is it usually faster or slower than yours? Is the depth of their breath deep or shallow? How does this compare to your breathing? Finally, where in the body do you notice the breath? This could be high in the chest, in the middle of the chest or possibly lower in the abdomen. You can notice the *location* of the breath based upon the rising and falling of the chest or abdomen.

People who are in deep rapport are seen to have matched breathing patterns. Thus, it is possible to develop rapport with someone by deliberately matching the person's breathing. I am not advocating that you match any unusual breathing patterns such as panting or rapid breathing, just match normal breathing.

> Try this exercise the next time you are sitting relaxed on the sofa watching TV with your spouse / partner. Match his/her breathing for two minutes (this is called pacing in NLP). Then breathe faster and watch to see if they start to breathe faster as well (this is called leading).

I use pacing and leading to create a sense of relaxation in clients. There are times when a client has just arrived at my office in a tense state, typically breathing very shallowly. As soon as we are seated I match their breathing for 30 seconds or so, then I take a deep breath and ease back into my chair. Almost immediately, the client mimics my breathing and eases back in their chair as well, becoming relaxed also.

One of the most interesting applications where I have used pacing and leading is during hypnosis. As a certified hypnotherapist, a large part of my training involved understanding how to assist a subject under hypnosis to remain calm and relaxed. Matching their breathing pattern is one of the most effective techniques for helping them. If I notice the subject start to breathe faster, I first pace their breathing for a moment, then I take an deep, audible breath, sometimes with a sigh, and then say the words *"Feel yourself sinking deeper and deeper into relaxation"* while continuing to breathe deeply. It works magically in calming the subject's breathing rate.

For those of you who are a bit shy to use some of the other rapport techniques we have discussed, matching the person's breathing can be the most subtle behaviour, and very hard for other people to detect. This technique takes practice, especially finding a way to notice the person's breathing *rate*. The easiest way is to watch the person's shoulders which will show the rhythm of the breathing.

Use small talk (phatic communication) to build rapport

Recently, I was hired by an organization to teach networking skills to a group of undergraduate engineering students from India and Brazil. The workshop I designed included a number of experiential exercises. One of these was to have them practice "**small talk**." It was interesting to find out that many had not heard of the term before. I explained that small talk is an expression for any informal dialogue that has no functional purpose other than to generate interest in each other to continue having a conversation. I suggested that they could begin by talking about the weather or the meal they were having. It was fun to see that they immediately understood what I meant and to watch as they began to practice small talk with each other.

Another term that has been used for small talk is **phatic communication** which can be verbal or non-verbal. The term phatic (from the Greek *phanein*: to show oneself) describes expressions that are used as a courtesy rather than to convey meaning or information. A simple *Hey, what's up, Have a nice day* or *How are you* are all examples of verbal phatic communication. Examples of non-verbal phatic communication can be *waving hello, thumbs up sign,* or even a *nod* to acknowledge someone.

Some social styles might find it more difficult to make small talk. Blues tend to be serious and want to stick to business. Reds don't want to waste time with what they feel is irrelevant chatter. Greens usually wait to be approached. That leaves the yellows, who I believe are the most natural at small talk. These are all generalizations, so these general rule may or may not be true for you. I believe phatic communication is a vital part of human communication since it opens the door to a social connection that can eventually lead to more substantive discourse.

Everyone should develop a level of proficiency in making small talk. Here are a few tips:

1. You need to know about current events and the news. Read as much as you can (newspapers, magazines, internet news) and listen to the news; watch TV or review websites that summarize the day's events. Do a little channel surfing before you leave for work.
What's the weather going to be like?

    I remember attending a human resources conference where I began a small talk with a gentleman about the weather. Although it was a bright, dry winter day, I saw on the TV in my hotel room earlier that a big snow storm was on the way. He said he had no idea, but was happy that I was telling him about it because he really had to get back home since he had an important meeting the next day. We exchanged cards and he left shortly after lunch. A week later he emailed to thank me for our brief conversation, and told me that he'd made it home safely. A few months later the president of his company wanted a team building workshop. I was recommended and subsequently hired for the job.

2. Attend different cultural events. Go to museums, art galleries, live theatre, parades and local music festivals.

3. Food and travel are also great subjects for filling conversations. Where have you traveled? What are the

highlights of the places where you have been? People love to talk about their travels and favourite foods.

4. Now that you have lots to say, practice wherever you can. First practice on your family and friends, people you know. How well can you switch from subject to subject? Then practice at your local coffee shop, or with a neighbour. Finally, you can graduate to cocktail parties, conferences and networking events.

5. Be a great listener. What did the person just talk about that may become an important subject you can expand on? Ask the person to tell you more about their subject of interest. Show a sincere desire to learn more about what is important to them. If you have special knowledge you can add your ideas on the subject to the conversation.

6. Don't be afraid to be silent. Filling every pause with words might make you appear nervous. Sip your cup of coffee or wait for the other person to say something.

7. How else can you build your conversational repertoire? Remember that variety is good. The more you practice small talk, the greater your confidence and competence will develop.

Phatic communication / small talk are mentioned here as a casual way to begin establishing rapport that might lead to more meaningful conversations.

Therapeutic rapport

Therapeutic rapport is a crucial element for building a solid relationship between a client and a counselor, coach, or health practitioner. This type of rapport is created through the active demonstration of empathy and understanding by the coach, where the client then feels a sense of safety, trust and respect.

Matching behaviour such as tone, speed of speech and volume of speech are subtle ways to begin building therapeutic rapport. Often slowing down the speech and speaking more quietly can generate a sense of calm. When the client is relaxed it is easier to pace and lead. You can decorate and enhance your working environment to create a calm and relaxed environment. I use neutral colours, soft music and a water fountain in the coaching area. I have had numerous clients who have expressed that as soon as they enter the location, they feel the stress draining away and a wave of calm, relaxing energy drift over them.

Empathetic listening is a highly effective method for generating therapeutic rapport. Empathetic listening is a way of listening and responding to the client that enhances mutual understanding. The client feels that you have accurately heard and interpreted what they are trying to convey. When people feel that you are empathetic, they feel comfortable in sharing their true feelings. Empathetic listening causes more information to surface as the counselor and the client explore and problem-solve together.

Empathetic listening (similar to Active Listening)

In empathetic listening, you transcend your own thoughts and emotions so that you can place yourself in the other person's shoes. Empathy is the capacity to perceive and understand the emotions of another as if you *were in their shoes*. Can you see things the way they see things? As if you were replaying the experience yourself? Can you feel what they're feeling? Can you shift your perspective to theirs?

Eight Steps that Form the Process of Establishing Empathetic Listening:

1. Empathetic listening requires that you *pay full attention* to the person in front of you. You cannot be looking at your smart phone or computer screen because this will instantly give them the impression that they are not important to you. Your undivided attention will help you to pick up on the emotional and factual content of their message.
2. Match their breathing if appropriate (i.e. the person is not panting or has other irregular breathing)
3. Always allow the person to *complete what they are saying without interruption*. Keep track of information by writing things down if you need, but allow them to speak.
4. Ask clarifying questions that expand on what they are saying. Ask what, when, where, how and who questions. Be careful of *why* questions since these lead to justifications and reasons that might send them into a cognitive loop that keeps them stuck trying to figure out why.
5. Use encouraging and neutral phrases such as *I see, please continue*, and *I believe I understand*.
6. Ask permission to summarize what you have heard and your understanding of the issues once they stop speaking. Be sure to use as many of their exact words (i.e. from your notes) when you talk about what you have heard. This is strategic because you become a

mirror, echoing their words back to them. I have found that clients are often surprised to hear back exactly what they have said. The repetition serves to help their self-discovery, in that they develop a greater understanding of the issue than they originally thought.
7. Express to them the feelings and emotions you are picking up from what they are saying. Ask them for validation.
8. Lastly, restate in your own words when you talk about your understanding of the situation and what you believe might be a possible solution. Or you can ask them what they think could be a solution. I always use provisional language at this stage, since it is important not to dictate solutions to the client. I usually say *"A possible solution might be..."* or *"Do you think this might work?"*

When I build therapeutic rapport with someone it happens quite quickly. This is probably a result of years of practice. I notice myself gently matching posture, facial expressions and breathing. At times it feels as if the person's emotions are contagious because I have such a strong sense of their feelings. It is very difficult to put into words the feeling of being in deep rapport with another person while still maintaining a healthy, ethical boundary.

I have been accused of reading minds. Clients say that my description of their situation seems unusually accurate. I don't believe I am reading their minds I believe that therapeutic rapport is the reason. In actuality, I experienced a flash of images, a mind-picture of parts of what they were relaying to me, which would help guide my questions as we explored the issues troubling them. I believe that therapeutic rapport assists in creating these deep connections.

Will I be Noticed Mirroring and Matching?

I am constantly asked "What if you get caught mirroring someone? Will they get upset that you are mimicking them?"

My response is simply that most people are not aware when they are being mirrored or matched. Whenever you mirror or match someone, their subconscious mind notices and sends an internal message that says, *"You are just like me, so I like you."* The person becomes relaxed and receptive to what you are saying and gets engaged in the conversation. Their conscious mind rarely notices what you are doing, especially if you wait at least 4 seconds before you mirror the person. As you continue, you should vary the duration of this wait time so as not to establish a pattern that is noticeable.

Your behaviour will bypass their conscious mind. People don't pay attention to microbehaviours. Individuals who are engaged in a conversation find that everything is contributing to the experience; people don't tend to break down our actions into separate components such as tone, gestures, posture and words, so it is unlikely they will notice you matching them.

As you master these hidden skills of building rapport, I recommend that you keep your movements smooth and as natural as possible. Don't make abrupt changes or odd facial expressions. Take your time, be yourself and keep a genuine smile.

I also advise you not to match or mirror idiosyncratic behaviours that are related to a person's disability, or unique gestures that are too obvious. Try not to force it – sometimes you have to build the rapport in small doses. Finally, don't be afraid to mirror and match others. Until you become more proficient, you might want to focus on matching rather than mirroring. That is, you can just approximate the behaviours you observe with similar movements.

When I look up the word Rapport, I found the following meanings:

> *1: relation of trust between people. 2: a feeling of sympathetic understanding 3: in accord, harmony. 4: having a mutual, especially a private, understanding.*

The techniques discussed here may seem manipulative, especially since you are doing something that the other person is unaware of. Yet if you review the definitions of rapport described here, you will see that with the right intention, rapport leads to more positive human interactions.

CHAPTER TEN

The Importance of Non-Verbal Communication

In the discussion on rapport building, we saw that a large majority of the techniques involved non-verbal components. Mirroring and matching tonality and body language plays a large part in establishing rapport with others. An American psychologist by the name of Dr. Albert Mehrabian was able to demonstrate the importance of non-verbal communication in a study where he developed what is now called the 7%-38%-55% rule.

In this rule, the 7% refers to words, 38% refers to the tonality and 55% refers to body language. Mehrabian studied the importance of verbal and non-verbal communication, and found that effective and meaninful communication about our feelings requires that these three components are congruent. In situations where there is ambigiuity between our words, the body language and our tone (i.e. when our verbal and non-verbal elements do not match), people will most likely trust the non-verbal information.

Mehrabian determined that non-verbal communication is significantly more important for communicating feelings and attitude, whenever the words we are saying are mismatched with our tone of voice. In situations where we are sending mix-messages between body and words, people will always use tone and physiology to determine our true feelings. In these cases, the non-verbal data makes up 93% of the meaning about how we feel, while the words represent 7%.

You have probably encountered a person who is trying to hide their emotions, but their tone and gestures give away their true feelings. You might ask them why they are upset and the turn to you and snap, "I'm not upset, everything's fine," as they jerk their body away from you. This is a classic example of what I am referring to here – the inconsistency between body, tone and words that causes us to dismiss someone's words altogether.

Not all examples of inconsistencies are this dramatic. There are times when we must watch for much more subtle incongruencies. We need to become good at noticing minute shifts in someone's facial expressions, body movements and even breathing. I refer to this as deep listening. **Deep listening** is a process that requires you to become hyper-vigilant at watching for and noticing tiny shifts in a person's behaviour and language. I use the word **micro-behaviours** to refer to the breaking down and describing of small changes in a person's actions such as shifting their posture, turning their head, yawning unexpectedly, sighing, rolling their eyes, that might indicate a shift in their normal pattern of communication. Once you notice these micro-behaviours, you will need to determine if it means something more than the person just shaking off muscular tension.

Dr. Paul Ekman, an American clinical psychologist, offers us a taxonomy for understanding and categorizing human emotions and facial expressions. He is considered a leading pioneer in the study of facial microexpressions. **Microexpressions** are involuntary facial expressions which appear based upon the emotional state of the person. These expression are very brief, lasting only factions of a second, and are hard to see without practice and training.

Ekman's research supported the idea that facial expressions of emotions are universal and not based on any specific culture. In his initial study, anger, disgust, fear, happiness, sadness and surprise were found to be universal emotions.

In a study of 20,000 people, Ekman discovered that only 50 could detect deception in the subjects. Along with Wallace V. Friesen, Ekman developed the Facial Action Coding System (FACS) in 1978 to categorize human facial microexpressions. The study looked at many of the muscle groups in the human face. The system defined the contraction and relaxation of one or more facial muscle groups. The final FACS manual was over 500 pages and it is now used for many applications – lie detection, psychology and even television series.

The television series *"Lie To Me"* is based upon the work of Paul Ekman. The taxonomy of facial expressions and their anatomical equivalent are used in the TV series as clues for figuring out when people are deliberately trying to hide their true feelings. Remember how we discussed earlier that a real smile will create crow's feet at the corner of the eyes. Ekman's research substantiates the Duchenne smile.

The FACS system has been developed into certification workshops where people go to learn the techniques of reading mircoexpressions. If you were an expert in FACS, you would have a distinct advantage over many others in your ability to read people and their true emotions. You could use the knowledge you gained from reading a person's microexpressions to build rapport and to better connect with them on a more genuine level.

Dr. Ekman was very gracious to give me permission to use the standardized faces depicting typical human emotional for a study I worked on with a neuropsychologist at the Clark Institute. We were studying how accurate and how quickly individuals with personality disorders could identify different facial emotions. Our hypothesis was that individuals who suffer from a personality disorder would take longer and make more errors than a normal population (the control group). Our initial findings were proven correct – indeed, individuals with personality disorders did take longer and had a greater number of errors when compared to the control group.

Facial expressions are only one of the many non-verbal behaviours that you need to pay attention to in order to communicate more effectively. When you are looking at body language, you need to look at variety of cues to figure out the accurate meaning in what you are observing. This is especially true when body language is not matched to the verbal language.

To demonstrate this lack of congruency, I want you to visualize someone standing in front of you, shoulders slouched, voice lowered, eyes and head down as they say *"Oh, I am really excited to be here."* This is a somewhat dramatic example, but I'm sure you can picture it right away. There's no doubt that the speaker is definitely *not* excited, because there are several non-verbal cues that scream boredom or apathy. This sort of ambiguity is what we need to look for when we suspect that someone is not really sincere in their verbal expression. Until you are an expert at micro-expressions, reading others will require that you become good at noticing and interpreting more macro physical activity.

There are a number of macro behaviours that are a natural part of human expression. Sitting in a boardroom, you can look around the table and see people who are folding their arms or legs, people tapping on the table, touching their hair, leaning one hand on their chin, scratching their head, clasping their hands together and more. The majority of these behaviours are subconscious, and the person is not aware doing them. Plan to focus on these behaviours throughout the week. Building physiological rapport is only possible if you have noticed the gestures you need to match.

> List some of your habitual non-verbal behaviours:

Another non-verbal behaviour is expressed in a person's posture. Posture can express a variety of things about someone. A woman has just arrived at an office for an interview. She stands erect, with her head up, and walks directly up to the receptionist to introduce herself, placing her card on the table to announce that she is there for the 2 pm interview. What impression do you think she will make on the receptionist? Does she appear confident and credible? If you said yes, you are correct.

What if there was another person who did all the same things, except their shoulders and head are slightly drooped and they're not making eye contact. They still announce their name, place their card on the table and so on. What do you think now? Do you think this person appears as confident as the previous person? Probably not! You can see how important posture is in conveying self-assurance, which is important whether you are entering a board room or walking onto a stage.

Reading Body Language

Developing a solid foundation for reading body language is an indispensable component in all aspects of communication. Whether you are about to do an interview, have a meeting and or participate in negotiations, understanding body language can give you the winning edge.

Words are easier to control than body language, which is harder to fake. When we have a certain thought, our subconscious produces automatic non-verbal responses that are out of our control. This was discussed earlier when we spoke about micro-expressions. Therefore, paying careful attention to nonverbal cues not only helps you determine sincerity, it also helps you to interpret and appropriately respond to the speaker's underlying attitudes.

In order to use body language as an accurate predictor of underlying feelings, you need to observe a series of gestures and facial expressions in conjunction with one another. You need to look for consistent combinations of clues appearing together before you can come to a specific conclusion about what you think is a person's true state-of-mind. The following chart provides a specific example of body language and its potential meaning. You can use this to determine when someone's verbal and non-verbal behaviours are incongruent. Use this cautiously, since it is a generalization. Your predictions will be more accurate if you combine and compare this information with the person's tonality.

Body Language and Possible Meanings

Body Language	Possible meaning
Leaning forward in a chair	Interested and attentive
Direct eye contact and smiling	Positive thoughts
Hands on chin and	Thinking / processing

leaning forward	what was said
Eyes wide, direct eye contact, warm smile	Willing to listen, objective, open
Direct eye contact and firm handshake	Confident and self-assured
Upright posture, direct eye contact, relaxed lips	Serious and paying attention
Leaning back in the chair; crossing arms and pursed lips	Disbelief and hostility
Crossing arms and legs and not smiling	Closed, defensiveness or lack of interest
Head leaning on cheek, elbow on the table leaning arm on table / holding head down	Boredom, fatigued, lack of interest
Gazing off in the distance and / or lifting their head up	Lack of concentration OR internally processing
Fidgeting and wringing hands	Lack of agreement
Fiddling with a pen and looking away	On a mental break;
Tapping fingers or feet, frowning, getting out of their chair and pacing	Frustration or impatience
Raising of eyebrows and widening of eyes	Surprise
Tense jaw and wide eyes	Irritated or exasperated
Touching or squeezing ears and avoiding eye contact, lips pursed	Disbelief

CHAPTER ELEVEN

Conversational Self-Defense

It was a very happy day for me when I discovered that people who got upset with me didn't necessarily want me to fix the problem, but often just wanted to be heard. Up until then, my typical response had been to try to rush the person through the conversation until I could figure out how to sort it out, and move on. In my mind, it seemed logical that if one was going to complain about something, they had to be looking for a solution. *Wrong!* Many people just wanted a chance to express their feelings and receive acknowledgement before any thought of a solution entered their mind.

As I learned more about handling difficult conversations, I discovered that it was my own desire to avoid conflict that had caused me to feel compelled to hastily push through all the gushy feelings and get to something concrete that we could *do* about the problem. It was pure avoidance. But the problem with avoidance was that people felt I didn't care and that they were arguing with a brick wall.

The truth is that I cared deeply, but felt that not engaging in the argument was a better solution than getting into a heated discourse. Wrong again! Lack of engagement was just the opposite of being on the offensive and firing a flurry of words. An angry outburst or silently withdrawing are both equally unhealthy reactions to an issue. It was clear that I needed to learn a healthier way to have a difficult conversation, and to develop a better form of conversational self-defense.

The Prescription

If you are learning any form of martial art self-defense, you are taught in your first class that you need to be in a relaxed, assertive, grounded, self-aware and clear-headed state. This is the opposite to being defensive. **Defensiveness** is characterized by being off-balanced, flustered and under emotional hijack. As in physical self-defense, **conversational self-defense** is the antidote for difficult conversations and it can be broken down into the following required elements.
You need to:
1. Remain emotionally-controlled and grounded
2. Stay self-aware of your contribution
3. Have mental clarity

Regaining Emotional Control

In our discussion on emotional hijack, we learned that when we feel threatened we devolve into an irrational state where our emotions take over and our mind shuts down. We are all aware that disagreements are at the top of the list of situations that push us into this emotional quandary.

In my many years of working with clients to overcome barriers to communication, I have discovered that most people will, at some point in their life, have at least one person with whom they have cyclical and ritualistic difficult conversations. Oddly enough, we are usually in a significant relationship with this person so it is not that easy to just walk away and ignore them. Even if we do choose to avoid them for a time, we will have moments where we have to think of how we can repair or rebuild the relationship or wondering if an apology is needed.

Cyclical hurtful conversations tend to follow a pattern. Let's say it starts with someone pushing you to an angry outburst. Shouting and swearing might ensue, along with hurtful words being exchanged. Before long, you or the other person has said or done something that you begin to wish you hadn't.

Once you have regained your composure, you may begin to feel guilty for treating the other person unkindly. But as you sit with the guilt and shame for your behaviour, your mind begins to replay all the reasons why you lost control. These justifications begin to well up in your heart and mind, thereby rekindling the initial anger which lays await under the surface, ready to be ignited again.

Our desire to avoid feeling guilty is a strong motivator for why the vicious **cycle of hurt** repeats again and again. *If only they didn't do what they did, I wouldn't have done/reacted the way I did.* You're stuck feeling a need to avenge the hurts of the past, and staying angry at someone else keeps you from feeling any self-blame for what you might have done to cause or escalate the argument in the first place.

The first step of conversational self-defense and for you to move beyond a difficult conversation is to regain control of your emotions. However, you have to really want to change, actively choose to notice the pattern, and interrupt it. As discussed, it is natural for you to feel justified in wanting to re-inflict the wound that you have received, but this only escalates the conversation to a greater level of intensity.

You can only exit the cycle of hurt by choosing to stop your angry outburst before it happens. It is only possible to keep cool if we are mindful and have a strategy to recover quickly from emotional hijack. This strategy was covered in the chapter "Emotions get in the way."

Here's a brief review: in order to control the intensity of our emotions, we need to go through a process of calming the physical symptoms; we can breathe deeply, or perform mental calisthenics (i.e. tell yourself to stop the behaviour) in order to move back to a calmer state.

Once you are back in a grounded state and feel composed, you can think rationally to formulate your verbal defense and move away from the negative dialogue. If you have exchanged angry words, this is the time to apologize – before more hurtful things are said.

The challenge with difficult conversations is that people feel that saying sorry is a sign of weakness and that it makes them more vulnerable. Many people also feel that to apologize is to admit or agree that the other person is right. They are caught up in a *Win the Battle, Lose the War* mentality. But the reality is, this apology is not about being right or wrong – it is about taking personal accountability for your outburst and for behaving badly toward somebody else.

In actuality, it takes great strength to apologize in a heated exchange where the other person might have also said things to hurt you. Even if you don't feel entirely at fault, you can still feel remorse for your contribution to the verbal attack and that the other person's feelings are hurt. Only those with a strong self-esteem find it easy to make this apology without feeling diminished.

I have witnessed it many times – people unable to be rational and think through a problem when they are highly emotional. I'm not saying that you should avoid your feelings. Feelings need to be expressed and acknowledged. But also remember that once the feelings are in check, you and the person can both think more coherently.

Self-Awareness Helps You Notice Your Contribution

A strongly self-aware person is more likely to have the capacity to determine their contribution to an issue. We know that an important factor in difficult conversations is taking ownership for your part in the blame game. This can be easier said than done, because if you feel someone has wounded you, your first instinct is to focus on how you will make *them* see their wrong and apologize. Eventually they might be able to say sorry, but this is not usually possible until someone de-escalates or diffuses the situation. The likely person to make this shift is you. As you are reading this book, you are learning techniques that give you a better chance of being able to sort things through.

Analyzing your contribution requires that you reflect on the situation as if you were a witness sitting on the sidelines or hovering above. If possible, you should step away from the conversation. Go for a walk. Take a deep breath. Work on achieving a calm, grounded state. Reflect on your behaviour by asking yourself the following questions: Did you say something to trigger the situation? Was it your tone or body language? Did you raise your voice? These questions will help you to recognize your own input toward the disagreement.

In some cases, we exacerbate our own pain with what we say to ourselves, or with what we remember from the past that is related to the present subject matter.

I recall one story that was recounted to me by my friend James about how he was self-sabotaging because of his own internal dialogue. He had found his dream job, but within his first month he began to second-guess his ability to do the work. His insecurity started shortly after he submitted his first project status report. When he sat down to discuss the report, his boss asked him a number of questions about his project approach. James felt nervous about the questions and began to berate himself internally for not anticipating what he would be asked. He was able to hold it together and handle the questions well enough, such that at the end of the meeting his boss told him that he was doing a great job.

Instead of feeling good about the praise he had just received from his boss, James went directly back to his desk and began to replay the whole meeting back in his head, wondering what else he should or could have said. Forgetting all about the compliment, he started to internally put down his own methodology. I tried to imagine why he was so critical of himself, so I asked him "Why are you being so hard on yourself? Your boss evaluated the work and was happy with it."

James replied, "I don't believe my boss, he was just saying that to be nice."

"Why don't you believe him?" I asked. "Your manager is ultimately responsible for the project getting completed, so he wouldn't take the risk to just be nice if he did not believe in your method."

James pondered my question. "My manager asked me a whole bunch of questions as if he didn't trust me."

It intrigued me to realize that James felt that being asked questions meant a lack of trust, so I asked him to tell me why he had reacted this way.

After taking some time for internal analysis, James said, "Growing up, I was taught that you had to be prepared and do your work thoroughly. My father used to scrutinize my homework and I would get quite an earful if I skipped any steps. There are no shortcuts in life, he would tell me – which usually meant that I would have to redo my homework. I credit my dad for how successful I have been, so I've always looked at things this way. It's funny how much I over-analyzed this situation and blamed my boss. Now I realize I brought this on myself. I guess I have to learn when it is appropriate to analyze and when I shouldn't."

James blew things out of proportion with his over-analysis and his self-talk. He felt that his boss had put him down, and that by asking him all those questions he had somehow placed James' ability to do the job into question. Upon further reflection on the situation, James realized that it was his own thoughts and actions that had precipitated his negative feelings.

Self-reflection is a vital part of developing self-awareness and building your conversational self-defense. Talking about your contribution to a difficult conversation requires the use of *'I'* language, such as *"I realize that you felt upset because I arrived late, but I did call ahead."*

> Ask yourself the following questions:
> Is there a possibility that you have blown things out of proportion?
> Is there an internal identity issue that caused you to be hypersensitive to what was being discussed?
> What is *your* self-talk?

Next, we need to reflect on the other person's behaviour. Imagine disassociating from the situation momentarily, then replay the conversation in your head to see what aspects caused you to feel upset. This is the way to determine what specifically affected you.

Is it the person's tone? Is it what they said? Is it their facial expression or a gesture? You have to be specific to make any corrective measure meaningful. You need to be able to express what you want them to change explicitly, such as, *"Maybe you didn't mean for me to feel ignored, but when you shrugged your shoulders, grimaced and turned away, I felt that you didn't care. What were you trying to tell me with your actions?"*

We teach others how to treat us, and so it is up to you to set clear boundaries with the people around you. Help the other person to see their contribution to the problem. Remember that having a conversation about contribution is only possible if you both have emotional control. This means that both of you have expressed and acknowledged each other's feelings in a calm, non-confrontational manner.

Once this step is covered, you can review what you have discovered about your own contribution and then invite the other person to explore what they felt happened. Additionally, you should let them know about the specific things that hurt you and what you think is the remedy.

Our fears start with our self-criticism, self-judgment and negative self-talk. We actually prevent ourselves from moving forward and often get stuck in a pattern we can't break out of. But whenever we take the risk to learn new things, we open ourselves up to potential improvement, which boosts our potential for growth.

As you review your contribution to the argument, remember there is no failure, only feedback.

How can you really fail, if every time you have an experience, you gain the opportunity to see if the experience matches the standard you had set out for yourself? At its core, feedback helps us to improve our ability to reach our goals.

Mental Clarity

The final step in having effective conversational self-defense is to have mental clarity. We all know that we are more adept at navigating our way out of arguments when we are mentally coherent. During grips of conflict we can become irrational and illogical. It is likely that we will interpret the situation to be more threatening than it is in reality. Exaggerating the effect on our well-being and triggering the fight and flight response are common byproducts of an overly-sensitive mind.

The worst result of this state of mind is that we delete, distort and generalize even more than usual, causing a distortion in our interpretations and conclusions about what is happening to us. We are not able to illustrate our opinions effectively, nor are we capable of **objectively listening** to the other person. *Objective listening* is our ability to listen to someone else's ideas or opinions, be open to accepting another's ideas to be as valid as ours, and possibly choosing their idea over our own.

Do you think you are a very competent objective listener? Realize that this is an essential skill for effective conversational self-defense. Instead of trying to outwit the other person like an opponent, we need to become curious about why they think the way they think, or why they say and do the things they do. Instead, we tend to suffer from cognitive bias. **Cognitive bias**, the tendency to process and filter information through our own experiences, likes and dislikes, is especially prevalent during arguments. We become more and more incapable to accurately process what the other person is trying to make us understand.

Cognitive biases can serve us well when they are used as an adaptive mental shortcut, because they lead to more effective actions in given contexts, and enable faster decisions when faster decisions are of greater value. A good example of this type of bias might be your favourite colour – this helps you to quickly pick a new shirt in a store filled with many shirts of different colours. However, imagine if you go into a store with a limited selection of colours of which your favourite is not available; it might just take you much longer to choose a shirt.

Cognitive bias can lead to perceptual distortions, confused judgment or irrational interpretations. One form of cognitive bias that is worth mentioning is *attention bias*. In an **attention bias**, you pay attention to certain details more so than others due to what you value or believe. This is potentially what is happening in an argument, where we are predisposed to pay attention to what we expect to hear.

A few weeks ago I was doing some coaching work with a woman who was in the process of transitioning to a new job. We will call her Sue for the purpose of this example. Sue wanted to leave her job due to dissatisfaction. We discussed some of the experiences she had in her existing role to help define more clearly what the new job needed to look like in order for her to have greater job fulfillment.

She started out describing some of her subordinates. She felt that they were constantly uncooperative. She also talked about her manager, describing her as controlling and micro-managing. I asked her to describe previous jobs. It was not long before we saw a pattern emerging. Sue had left 4 jobs in the last 6 years, prior to which she had worked as a senior manager for 15 years. She said that she really missed her role as a senior manager, but her old company had gone out of business and she was now trying to find a similar role. The past four jobs were all as a supervisor and just didn't match the senior manager role.

Sue had a cognitive bias for her previous senior manager role. Every new job was being compared to the job she'd lost and nothing measured up. She also no longer had the same level of power in the last four jobs. Subordinates appeared uncooperative because she did not feel that she had the enough authority to direct their work. Her manager appeared controlling because Sue was now in a role where she did not have as much autonomy as before. Hence, every new job would quickly become unsuitable.

Sue recognized the pattern she was locked in. She *valued* the freedom to control her own work and enjoyed the authority and autonomy of directing others in her senior manager role. However, these requirements conflicted with her need for security and the reduced responsibility of the jobs she was getting. She needed to create a different criteria for her job hunt. Together we worked at defining her ideal job, and she moved past the grief she still felt for the loss of her old job. Three months later, Sue found a great role as a consultant for an organization in the sector she desired.

Sue's example teaches us not only about cognitive bias, but also about cognitive dissonance. **Cognitive dissonance** is the tension produced by holding two competing or conflicting thoughts in our minds at the same time. In Sue's case, her need for freedom competed with her need for security. Her need for authority conflicted with her need for reduced responsibility. This predicament created the anxiety and lack of fulfillment she was feeling in the new jobs. She had conflicting values that she needed to reconcile and prioritize before she could settle on the type of role that would work for her.

The phenomenon of cognitive dissonance was first discovered by Leon Festinger, who studied a cult that believed the earth was going to be destroyed by a flood. He observed what happened to its members when the flood did not happen, particularly the committed ones who had given up homes and jobs to work for the cult. While fringe members eventually acknowledged they had been fooled, truly committed members were much more likely to reinterpret the evidence to show that they were right all along (the earth was saved from destruction because of their faithfulness).

Cognitive dissonance can also refer to the discomfort that is felt due to the differences between what you know or believe and the new content you are learning. Cognitive dissonance causes us to resist what you are being told since the new contradicts with your existing beliefs. As you reject the ideas of the other person, you have now opened the door for a potential disagreement. You have to make space in your mind to accommodate the new information.

We see nations at war due to conflicting belief systems. We must be open minded enough to accept the possible truth of new information even if there is a discrepancy between what you are hearing and what you already know. Once upon a time people were told that the earth was flat, but one brave individual decided to test this theory. You too should look for evidence that provides validation to support new knowledge. This may just be the way to avoid having a clash of opinions.

Earlier we discussed how Sue had a values conflict with her manager. **Values conflicts** can cause cognitive dissonance within an individual and disagreements between individuals. **Values** are important and enduring beliefs or ideals shared by the members of a culture or family about what is good or desirable and what is not. Values exert major influence on the behavior of an individual and serve as broad guidelines in all situations.

I have seen many examples of values conflicts that resulted in difficult conversations among friends, family and co-workers. Our values drive our behaviour from deep within the subconscious. It is not always obvious when conflicting values are at the root of an argument because we don't tend to speak about values in every day conversations. Yet, drilling below the surface of our angst, we often will come up with conflicting values.

Many of Sue's disruptive conversations with her most recent manager were due to their values conflict. Sue really enjoyed the freedom and autonomy of being able to work on her own to make important decisions. But Sue's manager wanted to be kept in the loop each step of the way and needed to discuss each decision so she could provide her input. Neither side wanted to give up what they valued.

Once Sue understood the values conflict with her manager, she decided to increase her interaction with her. As Sue provided her manager with more information and opportunities for input, the less her boss demanded to be involved in every decision. Their relationship improved substantially. Sue triumphed over both her cognitive bias and cognitive dissonance to enable more constructive conversations.

Active listening as a Tool for Mental Clarity

An exploration of both sides of the story is required to make the most from a difficult conversation. Listening skills are the best tool you have for unraveling the web of misunderstandings. *Active listening* is a technique for listening and responding to another person that results in improved communication and understanding. In a previous chapter "The mind does the listening," we reviewed how the mind deletes, distorts and generalizes information. It is essential that the interpretation and evaluation of what we are hearing is as accurate as possible. When we actively listen, we have the best chance to facilitate mutual understanding.

Active listening – also called **paraphrasing** – provides many benefits to help you increase your communication effectiveness. With active listening others will feel that you are listening more attentively. You have an opportunity to verify your understanding of the speaker. It provides an active process for exploration of feelings and thoughts, and assists in creating acceptance of each other's views.

Active listening involves several steps. *The first step is to paraphrase or restate the main idea* of the speaker in your own words. Don't add too many extra words, be precise and to the point. Next, *share your understanding* of what you have heard. Avoid adding your own meaning to their words. Allow for a *pause* to give the *person the chance to agree, disagree or clarify* for mutual understanding. *Ask questions* to move past confusion. Another key step is to *reflect back the emotional content* of the message so the speaker knows that you understand how they feel, trying not to minimize or maximize the intensity.

To summarize, active listening involves:
1. Paraphrase the main point in your own words
2. Share your understanding of key ideas
3. Pause to allow the speaker to agree or disagree
4. Ask questions to clarify
5. Reflect back the speaker's feelings

These steps for active listening need to be practiced frequently until they have been perfected. Some of the steps may feel very unnatural and awkward at first, but practicing will make the process become smoother.

Final Rules of Engagement for Conversational Self-Defense

The following is a list of guidelines that you can follow to navigate your way out of a difficult conversation:

1. There is no right or wrong ... just different perspectives.
2. You may invite someone to discuss something you feel is important, but they may choose that this is not the right time or place for a discussion,
3. Avoid gossip and backstabbing. If someone starts to talk in a derogatory manner about a third party, don't get involved in their drama. If someone has a problem with another individual, suggest to them that they approach this person directly.
4. Don't use Emotional Hijack to intimidate or gain attention.
5. If you're not ready to discuss something, you may choose to "park" items.
6. When you think up a problem, also think of a solution that you can suggest to make things better.

CHAPTER TWELVE

Reframing: A Tool For Change

Reframing is a powerful tool for shifting our perspective. You've probably heard people talk about someone's "frame of reference", where the individual's perspective provides a context or focal point for their thoughts and actions. Imagine the function of a picture frame: it creates the borders for an image. This is analogous to the **frame** a person might use to set the parameters of how they choose to view the world. These frames are defined by your beliefs about yourself and others. If you narrow your frame with limiting beliefs, you will reduce what you see in a situation. These limitations can be observed in "I can't do that" self-talk or "You can't do that" judgment of others.

When you are in a self-limiting frame, you have strong boundaries that are used to keep out anything that does not fit within the frame. A lot of my life coaching work is with individuals who hold beliefs which prevent them from exploring possibilities that are outside their frame of reference. Phrases such as "I am not promotable", "I will never get over these feelings of rejection" or "I can't learn these things, I'm too old," are all examples of limiting beliefs that lock the person away from the opportunity to test if these thoughts could indeed be false.

Typically, people don't question if their beliefs are true or false. They accept their beliefs as fact, holding that what they tell themselves has to be true. Time and again, I have witnessed how frames keep people stuck and incapable of letting go of a past experience that often creeps into the interactions they have with others.

When we reframe our perspectives, we give ourselves the chance to see a situation from a different viewpoint. Reframing helps us to perceive, interpret, conclude and react to an experience in a different manner. Imagine being told that you have $200,000 versus $400,000 to buy an apartment – wouldn't it change your approach on where and what you might buy? What about if you were told you had one week to work on a report versus two days? This timeframe would impact your level of stress and the method you'd use to complete the report.

Reframing expands your potential by giving you another way to think, feel, do and ultimately choose how you will respond to an experience. By reframing, your new perspectives will create new possibilities.

You can see reframing examples all around you. Many years ago a good friend told me a story about how he got to replace his living room windows. He kept telling his wife that he wanted to replace the windows, but at the time they just did not have the money. He kept pondering how he might raise the funds, and suddenly one summer afternoon a fluke storm came out of nowhere. Heavy winds and a dark, ominous cloud loomed just above his and a neighbour's house a few acres away. Within minutes, a shower of large hailstones fell down upon the houses, shattering several windows. My friend said that it was the oddest thing. While assessing the damage in the aftermath, he and his wife lamented their bad luck and wondered what they were going to do.

As quickly as the storm came, a thought came to him – *we are insured for this kind of problem!* Yes, we can *actually replace those old windows with the insurance money!* A month or so later they had brand new living room windows. Instead of thinking of the storm as the enemy, my friend considered it his good fortune, especially as their insurance premiums did not increase. This is a powerful example of reframing. He later told me, "My neighbour failed to reframe, even though he also used insurance to install new windows. To this day he still complains about the terrible storm that broke all of his windows, and he relives the stress every time he tells the story."

When we reframe, we look at how we can assign a new meaning to an event. On August 14, 2003 there was a major blackout of power that affected around 10 million people in Ontario and 45 million across eight states in the U.S. I remember that day very well, because I had a technician installing a ceiling fan over a dining table. He had just gotten up on the ladder and was pulling out the wires of the old fixture, when all the lights and the stereo system went dead in my home office. I was not happy because I was trying to complete a report which needed to be printed. My immediate thought was that the guy had damaged the wires and zapped all the power in the apartment, so I walked into the dining room asking him what happened. He jumped off the ladder saying, "Don't know, I'll check the fuse."

A few minutes later we realized that the power was out in the entire building. I jokingly said to him, "Just wait until I tell them you did it."

It was a shocker to listen to my battery-operated radio and discover how widespread the blackout was. Power wouldn't be restored for hours, possibly days. Although we were initially upset, my family and I found it exciting to plan what we would do. We walked down nine flights of stairs and met up with many others who were headed down the street toward a line of restaurants and stores to buy extra food and water. It was a festival-like atmosphere as we reconnected with our neighbours, shared our flashlights and even the glow of our cell phones on the climb up the stairs back to our apartments.

The blackout gave us an opportunity to reframe our reaction. We could have felt angry about the inconvenience of having no power, but we changed what it meant to us and instead enjoyed the excitement of connecting with others in such a unique way. By changing the meaning, our response and feelings also changed.

As you can see, an event all on its own does not have innate meaning. We attach meaning to the events we experience due to our beliefs, values, biases and personal interpretations. You probably have heard of two people having the same experience but describing it completely differently. We discussed how this is possible in the chapter called "Reality is Relative."

When a police officer comes to an accident scene, his first task is to separate the witnesses. Then he/she will interview each witness separately. One witness says "It was a green car that sped through the intersection" and the other witness says "It was a blue car that sped through the intersection." The officer doesn't hesitate to record the incident as "a bluish-green car that sped through the intersection," because he/she realize that both individuals could be right.

So far we have been discussing **content reframing**, which answers the question *"What else could this mean to me?"* or *"In what way is this positive?"* We can also do **context reframing**. When we make a contextual change, we need to answer the question, *"In what context would this event or behaviour have value to me?"* If your best friend annoys you by never choosing the restaurants for outings, tell yourself *"Hooray, I get to pick what I want"* or *"They are easygoing enough to go along with my choice."* Trust me, the opposite can be worse – having someone who always wants to force their choice on you.

There are many applications of reframing in communication and counseling. These include:

- Difficult conversations
- Negative events
- Negative feelings and behaviours
- Limiting beliefs
- Options in negotiations
- Solutions to a problem

The Reframing Process

Reframing is one of the key tools described in detail by the founders of Neuro-Linguistic Programming, Dr. Richard Bandler and Dr. John Grinder, in their book *Frogs into Princes*. The process for reframing was described in six steps, which I have modified to be more applicable to reframing interpersonal interactions. Reframing can be achieved with the following procedures:

1. Start with self-reflection to determine what negative behaviour you want to change. How does this behaviour make you feel? This is the awareness stage.
2. Imagine you are talking to the part of yourself that is producing this unwanted response. What purpose does the behaviour serve?
3. Relax and see if something comes to mind. In the chapter on "Formative experiences" we discussed that many negative behaviours are driven from a sub-

conscious motivation that may have served a useful purpose or intention at some point in your past. This response may no longer serve you, however.
4. Now, brainstorm on a piece of paper what you believe are alternative responses or meanings you could apply to the situation. Is it possible to develop a new behaviour that still serves the useful purpose? Can you see how a new response will have a more resourceful or positive result? This is the time to consider if a content or context reframe is required.
5. Now evaluate each of the alternative responses. Which do you think would be the most natural and effective behavioural change that will help you to fully commit? You will need to allow yourself to accept a new perspective or response to the event in order to move past the old.
6. Finally, review how the newly selected responses and/or meaning will affect you and others. Does the reframe make you feel a greater sense of well-being?

How does the reframe affect those around you? The people closest to us can feel threatened when we change. We may become unpredictable to them, and so they might sabotage or resist our changes. Decide how you will notify others of your new choices so they are not suspicious. No one likes to be surprised when our loved ones appear too different. Let them know that you are reframing the way you think to become a more flexible person.

Choosing between two negative options

Often we are faced with the unpleasant task of choosing between two equally unwanted alternatives. Reframing can help you to make the best selection. If you have a task that you find undesirable, you should contrast it with the consequence of not doing it. The ultimate objective is to allow yourself to see that the consequence of not completing the task is much more undesirable than doing the task in the first place.

Say you dislike tallying up all of your receipts each month in order to submit your expense report, so you typically procrastinate until the last minute. Now, your company has just implemented a policy that expense reports must be submitted in the same month that the expenses occur. If you are like me, your first reaction is frustration about the new policy, but once you settle down you will recognize that the consequence of your procrastination will be a loss of money, because you can't be reimbursed until those receipts are handed in. Sometimes it's all about choosing the lesser of two evils.

Reframe the situation so that *you are* making the choice, rather than feeling like you are being forced to do something you don't want. This puts the situation back under your control and helps you to see things in a more positive light. You will feel more powerful if you *choose* to do something rather than if you feel you *must* do it.

Follow the scheme below to help you reframe:
- You are told that *you must do X*, but you have told yourself you don't want to
- So tell yourself that *if I don't do X, the consequence is Y*
- Therefore you willing *choose to do X to avoid the consequence Y*

Reframing can help to overcome negative events and have hope for the future. It can also help people to picture a future state that is positive. The following story illustrates a situation where reframing has helped a client to feel more optimistic.

A woman had just gone through a divorce and was feeling depressed about being a single parent and being alone. We used reframing to help her visualize a more positive future. She was not longer controlled by her ex-husband's choices for her. She imagined doing all the fun activities she now had time for that she couldn't do before, and going on trips to places where her ex-husband hadn't wanted to go to. Instead of focusing on her loss, she focused on the exciting new possibilities that lay ahead.

Reframing will help you to unlock your inner chameleon as you transform your negative self-talk into a more uplifting potential.

PART TWO

APPLICATIONS

Claudia Ferryman

CHAPTER THIRTEEN

Powerful Negotiations in Seven Steps

Over the past six years of polling students in my classes at the University of Toronto, I've noticed that four out of five students typically give me words with negative connotations when I ask them what they think when I mention the word *negotiation*. In a brainstorm exercise, a large majority of students will use words such as *adversarial, competition, win-lose, arguing, giving in* and *confrontation*. The rarer student will say *compromise, cooperation* and *conciliation.*

I am offering you the opportunity to reframe your perspective on negotiations. This reframing begins when you allow yourself to believe that negotiation is just a special type of conversation in which both you and someone else mutually desire a positive outcome. In the simplest terms, **negotiation** *is the process of communicating back and forth to reach a joint decision.*

If you are looking for a house to buy and you negotiate with a seller, you must recognize that both of you have a mutual desire: he/she wants to sell and you want to buy. What if you are negotiating a salary increase? Most people will say that their boss won't want to pay them more money. However, your boss does want you to be happy so that you don't leave – that is, if you are doing a good job. Even in this supposedly oppositional situation, you and your boss have similar objectives.

What if you wish for different or opposing objectives? The fact is that when we want different things, our desire can still lead to a good negotiated outcome. Two years ago, I counseled a couple who argued every time they started to plan their vacation. The husband wanted holidays where he could sit on the beach and enjoy pure relaxation, while his wife wanted to have adventures where she could experience different cultures and see museums. Their vacation planning often ended in an argument, as they equally felt their desires were mutually-exclusive. I prompted them to ask themselves if they could think of a vacations they'd had that had been both relaxing and adventurous.

At first we didn't get too far. Their mismatched tastes had gone on for so long that they kept thinking it was impossible to agree on something that would make them both happy. Eventually we brainstormed a number of possibilities, such as cruises, separate vacations and getting a camper. Finally, they decided on cruises. They saw that at sea they would be relaxing on board at the pool, and at each port the wife (or both) could go off on a more active adventure.

A powerful negotiator will always have a game plan and a strategic approach to making the negotiations successful. In this chapter you will learn the seven steps toward powerful negotiations, which are:
1. Identify your objective
2. Prepare and research
3. Brainstorm alternative solutions
4. Plan your approach
5. Set the right atmosphere
6. Make it a problem-solving discussion
7. Move to a close

Step 1: Identify your objectives

The first step in getting ready for negotiations is to determine what you want. What do you really, really want? Identify all the objectives up front. This will guide your preparation, planning, and ultimately your proposal. People can bring up more than one objective in a negotiation. A union, for example, might come to the table negotiating for their members a combination of reduced workflow, a raise, plus improved pension plans.

You may not have as many objectives, but be sure to think each one through systematically so you don't miss any. Afterwards, go through and prioritize them, weighing each in order of importance. You should always know which objectives you are willing to give up if you need to make concessions.

Write down each objective as a succinct sentence, as seen in this example:
1. Gain an increase in salary (between 15 – 20%) in recognition of my contribution to the organization
2. Negotiate for an extended benefits program
3. Arrange for flex time. I will work later during the week so that I will get half-day Fridays during the summer months.

Notice that each item is sequenced in priority order. Also, item one is already written as a percentage range. When you think about numbers such as a salary increase you want to have a range that covers three criteria:

1. First is your ideal wish – in this case 20%
2. The second number will be the most realistic or plausible (you might get 17%)

3. Third will be the minimum you will accept. This number might actually be 12%, but notice I wrote 15% as the lowest number in the range. You want to keep your minimum number secret this way you have room for negotiations.

Another way to understand you priorities is to review what you *want* versus what you *need*. Your needs are things you cannot do without. Everyone would advocate that we all need more money, but maybe a CEO who is earning a few million dollars annually doesn't really need the additional half-a-million dollar bonus. You have a really great working cell phone, but all the ads have you wanting the new smart phone. You can do without it, but your preference is to have it because all the cool kids are getting it. When you write your objectives determine which are *needs* and which are *wants*. We will have more flexibility around our wants than our needs.

The next outcome you need to think about is related to the opposition. What are their objectives? A great negotiator anticipates what would please the opposition. What would they want or need? What are the alternatives you could offer in place of these? Make your best guess and strategize how you could meet their objectives.

Once you have your objectives sorted out, it is time to prepare your case.

Step 2: Prepare and research

Preparation and research are absolutely essential for excellent results in negotiations. The major areas to focus your preparation are:
    a. Do your research
    b. Assess the opposition

c. Sharpen your skills for communication and negotiation

Research all aspects of the potential deal.
What if you are negotiating a salary for a new position – do you know if your expectations are realistic? Knowing the typical salary ranges that the organization offers for such a position would be a great asset in helping establish your desired salary ahead of the negotiations. This means that you need to gather business intelligence about the company and its salary history. You could talk to previous employees or search for the many sites on the internet that list company and salary information.

If you are making a purchase, you need to analyze and compare the pricing and options of the product you about to buy. Is there a store with an overstock of the item you desire, they will be more willing to give discounts? What day is the slowest day at that store? When are they receiving new inventory? When is the salesperson's quota cycle? Having this information will give you a leveraging point during bargaining.

Look at the comparables for the house in the neighbourhood you are about to put an offer on. How motivated is the seller? The sellers of the first house I bought were an elderly couple who had already purchased their retirement condo and were paying high maintenance fees. This was a great piece of information for me in the negotiations because I knew they were very motivated to sell to avoid paying two mortgages. I offered them a 30-day closing and they were happy to accept my offer.

Assessing the opposition
This is an essential step in your pre-negotiation preparation. Don't be shy to ask who will be involved in

the meetings, including their names and positions in the organization. Will these individuals have the authority to close the deal with you directly, or will they have to go to someone else for approval? Deferring to someone in authority is a widely-used tactic many negotiators and salespeople use to alter the agreement on certain commitments once you've already been psychologically invested.

Deferring to higher authority is a gambit that is used often in negotiations. A **gambit** is an opening action (strategy or tactic) or remark that is calculated to gain an advantage. A word that is commonly used in chess where the player has a planned series of moves at the beginning of the game such as an opening move in which a player makes a sacrifice (usually a pawn) for the sake of a compensating advantage. Simply put, a gambit is a trick to manipulate the outcome of the negotiations.

I had the fortune of attending a negotiation program run by Roger Dawson, a renowned authority on negotiations. In his book *Secrets of Power Negotiations* he wrote about the best counter-gambit to deferring to authority. He said that your first approach should be trying to remove the other person's resort to higher authority before the negotiations even start, by getting him to admit that he could make a decision if chose to go ahead with the proposal.

This is a standard practice in car dealerships. The salesperson takes you for the test drive, talks about options and gains your commitment with reduced pricing. The final moment comes for your signature, but the salesperson says, "I just need to get my manager to approve all the discounts." While you are waiting, you are already imagining yourself coasting down the highway with your

400 watt speaker system turned to the max, only to be told a few minutes later that the $200 off was not approved. What do you do? Chances are, you're going to agree anyway because you are now emotionally invested in those amazing speakers. Instead, what you should have been doing is asking the sales guy if he has final authority to approve the deal, and if not, ask to also deal with the person who has the final say. You can always shop somewhere else if they won't cooperate.

Learn as much about the circumstances and preferences of the individuals you will be meeting. Are they known to be difficult negotiators, or are they likely to be cooperative? Will they want to avoid conflict like those with a High Steadiness factor (Greens) or will they be very assertive such as those with a High-Dominance factor (Reds)? Will they want a lot of details (Blues) or will they take you off track on tangents during the discussion (Yellows)?

If you're going to apply for a raise, you should be analyzing your manager's communication profile. Create a profile based upon the foundational tools you have learned in this book. Can you find out their DISC Communication style and their learning style? The more you know about the person you will be negotiating with, the easier it will be to build subconscious rapport with them. This rapport will help you to establish a trusting connection, which in turn will pave the way for smoother discussion.

Here are some of the questions you should answer about the opposition:
1. Are they a strong, experienced negotiator?
2. Are they introverted or extroverted?

3. Are they visual, kinesthetic, auditory or auditory digital?
4. Are they accommodating or assertive?
5. What's the best way to build rapport with them?
6. What are their strengths and possible weaknesses?
7. Do they have access to information or facts that you don't have?
8. Do they have the power and authority to do the deal?
9. Are they under a time pressure that you can use to your advantage?
10. What do you think they want out of the negotiations?

In addition to reviewing all the foundational communication techniques and tools, you must also prepare yourself mentally. A well-prepared negotiator has the courage to ask for what they want and have the patience and stamina to take their time to outlast the opposition.

Negotiation will also test your ability to live with ambiguity. How long can you live with not knowing the outcome? If you have a high need to control and/or you are impulsive, you will not perform well in negotiations. You will also be at a great disadvantage if you don't have emotional restraint. Review the tools for overcoming emotional hijack in the chapter "Emotions get in the way."

Step 3: Brainstorm alternative solutions

Brainstorming is an effective way to generate lots of possible solutions and to evaluate the best among these ideas. It is important that you are not uptight when brainstorming. Get into a relaxing and creative state and don't limit yourself by thinking your ideas are unrealistic. Collaborate with a trusted friend or colleague as you conjure up other alternatives and options to meet your objectives. Most people are aware of the formal process of brainstorming, so here is a brief overview of the steps:

1. List the objective for which you are seeking possible alternative outcomes
2. Think of a question to stimulate thinking, such as, *"In what ways might we reach a solution?* or *What alternative offers will I find more agreeable than this one?"*
3. Give yourself a time limit, say 25 minutes, to think of at least 10 to 20 alternatives to the objective
4. Use a piece of paper with two columns and write these alternatives down as fast as you can in column one. It is important to not get critical as the ideas are flowing – just write it all down without evaluating them
5. Review all the ideas and score them from 1 to 5, where 1 is low-realistic and 5 is highly realistic. Then cross out all the 1s to 3s.
6. Now look at the 4s and 5s and rank them in order of your preferred outcome

There is a possibility that you will not get everything you have outlined in your objectives. Therefore, you need to have a number of additional options and ideas as alternative demands. Brainstorming alternative outcomes prior to the negotiations is the best way to prepare for potential variations in what you ask for versus what you are offered.

What else might you be willing to accept in lieu of your original proposal? Instead of the full salary increase you request, if the company offers to pay for additional training as part of the offer would you be ready to respond? Would this be an acceptable substitute? You would have the advantage of prior thinking if this was one of the options on your brainstorming list. You would already know how you feel about this possible alternative, thus be in a position to respond on the spot.

Look for options that will be mutually-beneficial for all parties. What might they want that you also want? In the case of a compensation package, for instance, paid training is a great component that provides benefits for you and the employer.

Step 4: Plan your approach

Your approach needs to be flexible. Negotiations don't typically follow a specific sequence even with the best pre-planning. The other participants are coming with their own ideas of the process, which may not match yours. There are lots of things that could change at the last minute, including the people, the location, and what is being offered.

Due to the unpredictable nature of negotiations, you should write down everything that you planned and prepared, including the main proposal, the numbers, profile of the opposition and so on. These will be your briefing notes that you will reference prior to the meetings. I don't take this document with me into the meeting, I leave it in the car, just in case it gets lost, I would not want the opposition to see my notes. I usually take a summary of these notes with just the main points into the meeting.

Draft a proposed agenda for the meeting, with each item for discussion listed in priority order. Design the agenda to have easy, non-controversial topics at the beginning, harder topics in the middle, and simple discussion or wrap-up topics at the end. I generally recommend that the negotiation not run longer than 2 hours each time you meet. If the meeting has to go longer, you need to take a 15-minute break every 90 minutes or so.

You strategically place easy items at the top of the agenda. These should be items that you already agree upon and feel you have as a common ground. This is a psychological tactic to make everyone feel closer together rather than further apart. I have seen people in negotiations spend little time talking about what they've already agreed upon in order to save time, but this is a step that is crucial in building a positive momentum.

You need to discuss the harder topics in the middle because you build on the positive energy of the earlier items, and if someone is late to the meeting, it would buy time until they arrive. Use the last part of the meeting to summarize and clarify items. Follow the additional agenda-planning guidelines found in the chapter on meetings.

Roles need to be defined if you will have more than one person on your side. You won't want to have one team member tripping over the next in the meeting. The first step is to appoint a leader of the group prior to going into the negotiation. This person will coordinate your side of the meeting, including calling upon other team members at the appropriate time. The leader is usually the most experienced negotiator in the group and is responsible for summarizing and announcing final agreements.

You will usually have two tactical players – the good guy and the bad guy. The good guy will come across as very relaxed and will be outlining points of agreement; he's the empathetic listener who will express understanding. The bad guy will remind others where agreement has not been reached, and why an agreement must be achieved.

Brainstorming options with the opposition is one of the most advantageous techniques for getting past a barrier to moving forward. Be prepared to propose this as a step in the process. Recall that you always separate the idea generation stage from the evaluation stage in brainstorming. This is your opportunity to bring forward some of the ideas you came up with during Step 3, that you feel may present alternative options for the other side.

Write up the key points of your proposal to use as a guide during the meeting. Include any supporting statistics, market research or competitive analysis that you need to support your objectives.

Step 5: Set the right atmosphere

Setting the right tone for the negotiations is critical. There are many components that go into creating a neutral setting where you can build a positive interaction. This has a lot to do with your attitude and emotional state as well as where you have the meeting. The two things you are encouraged to do are:
    a.   Tame your ego and control your emotions
    b.   Select a suitable location and seating plan

Ten years ago I was negotiating for a senior role in a mid-size information technology company. The Branch Manager was very eager to close the deal prior to leaving for meetings in another city and he wanted to bring home the news that I was on board. We had a week before he had to leave town. The deal was very amiable for me, except the contract stipulated that I could not continue any additional business after I took the new job.

I had a lucrative side business developing websites and did not want to divest it, so I made changes to the contract and there were many discussions back and forth about my ability to handle the new role, plus continue my other business. I waited until just hours before the Branch Manager needed to go. Being in a rush, he finally agreed to allow the changes in the contract before leaving for his flight. I had utilized both patience and the pressure of time as negotiation gambits in this situation. This example illustrates the importance of maintaining emotional control and having staying power, which is so crucial in helping your side.

Recently, real estate agents have benefitted from the hype in the housing market. Specifically, a concept called a *bidding war* or *bidding party* has been introduced to leverage potential owners' emotional and impulsive reactions. In a bidding party, agents set it up so that buyers cannot bid upon a home until a specified time and date. This forces individuals to make multiple offers on the home. This works well for sellers because the emotional buyer is likely to offer a large sum, blindly, in hopes of outbidding everyone else. It is not surprising to see offers far in excess of their listing price.

If you walk into negotiations already emotionally invested, it could lead to an **escalation of commitment** which may cause you to make irrational decisions. The opposition may take advantage of your weakness. An escalation of commitment is the tendency to put in more and more resources in an obvious losing proposition due to the time, effort, emotions and money that you have already invested.

Determining the location for the meeting is an important step. Often times you might be encouraged to have the negotiations on the opposition's turf, but it is important to try to get agreement upon a neutral location. This gives each party an equal footing so there's no home turf advantage. The only drawback is that you will need to arrive much earlier to review the setup and select your seat. If you meet at your own location, there are advantages in that you have more control of the environment, but it is harder to get people to leave. If you meet at the opposition's location, you are out of your comfort zone and cannot be certain about distractions or interruptions. The advantage of meeting in their location is that you can defer items because you are not at your office, as well as leave if you want.

Arrive early and choose a seat cater-corner to the leader of the opposition. This seat gives you a psychological advantage. The physical proximity will help you and the other person to feel closer together, rather than sitting across the table from each other which might make you feel like adversaries. Place each chair an equal distance apart around an oval or round table if possible.

Provide refreshments and then hang out with the other team. Sharing a coffee and a quick snack with the opposing team is a great way to begin building rapport. Exchanging a bit of small talk relieves tension and reduces their defenses. This is the time to observe the other team to determine their representational system, body language and tone, and their DISC Communication Style. Humanizing the negotiations will pay off when the process hits a roadblock. Mirror and match behaviour. If they are very serious, you should keep it more formal. If they are informal, match this approach.

Step 6: Make it a problem-solving discussion

Open the meeting by thanking the other party for meeting. Let them know that you value their time and look forward to working things out together. Use *we* language as much as possible, such as *"I truly believe that we will jointly come up with a mutually-beneficial solution."*

Gain agreement on the proposed agenda. The items you have in common are a good place to start the discussion. Open the conversation by focusing on points of agreement, then progress gradually to more challenging points working toward resolving each along the way. Avoid confrontational dialogue. Discuss everything from the perspective of mutual problem-solving.

Pick the right seat. Sit confidently, with your shoulders and head up and an open posture. Make direct eye contact with each person in the room and remember to build subconscious rapport. If you are negotiating with a multi-person team, observe everyone to determine who might be the **primary decision-maker** – the person who has the final say. This is typically the person who everyone seems to be looking toward or deferring to during discussions. Subsequently, work to figure out who is the **key influencer** – this is the person the primary decision-maker consults on various aspects of the negotiations, or whom the decision-maker seems to listen to the most.

Scan the body language of the opposing team to determine their DISC Style so you will know who wants more or less details, who will need time for processing (internal processors), and who will want to talk it out (external processors).

Presenting the proposal

In your planning stage you would have decided if you're going to present the proposal first or wait for an offer from the other party. Sometimes both parties will come to the table with some key points of the negotiations. For instance, if you are working out a compensation plan, your manager might bring forward the key numbers for salary and commissions, and you might add to the wish list items you desire, such as benefits, paid training, parking space and other perks.

Typically I'll bring a brief summary of key points of my proposal which I might provide a copy of to the opposition, especially if I suspect they are visual or tactile. Be cautious of being too excited when you are reading the proposal, because it might give away that you are overly committed. Keep your emotions in check as you make your presentation.

Talk about the need for agreement early in the negotiations by saying something like, *"I am sure that we are all eager to see things move forward so that there won't be any delays in implementing this project. I'm ready to work with everyone here to develop a mutually beneficial solution."*

Additional opening statements could consist of, *"I have prepared an overview of some key points for discussion,"* or *"I am expecting to receive your input on the items I'm about to propose."* Use provisional language that provides room for feedback. Phrases such as, *Here's a possible solution,* or *Maybe this will work,* or *Can we consider...* all provide a sense of being open rather than closed. This means avoid definitive or conclusive words such as *no, never* or *absolutely.*

As you present your key objectives, leave yourself lots of space to bargain if it becomes necessary. This means presenting the numbers in ranges rather than giving specifics. If you need to review, go back to step 1 and follow the guidelines for setting out your objectives.

Speak deliberately, with confidence but not too quickly. Pause at the end to give the other person the opportunity to absorb what you are conveying and to ask questions for clarification. Answer all questions with a full response rather than just saying yes or no. As you respond with complete answers, you are modeling what you need back from your opposition since you also want them to give you full answers. The more information you get, the more content you will have to use toward reaching an agreement.

Whether you are presenting or receiving a proposal, don't agree too quickly to any offer. This could cause the other party to feel they could have offered you less or they could have asked for more. Also, avoid making too many concessions early in the negotiations. Work on expanding options and brainstorming other solutions before giving up any substantial components of your proposal.

Overcoming barriers to agreement

People can also play tricks during the negotiations in order to gain the upper hand or control the process. Don't be surprised if the other side becomes uncooperative at times. One such tactic is called **stonewalling**, which includes delaying or stalling the proceedings, refusing to answer each question, or walking out on the discussion. The intention behind stonewalling is to force you to give in, or at least feel intimidated enough to back off on some of the items in your proposal. If you suspect stonewalling is taking place, you need to bring this up straight away so that the other party knows that you are not willing to continue negotiations if the behaviour persists. If you allow stonewalling to go on for too long, the other side might begin to believe that it's a viable tactic, and they may hunker down and continue using it. One way you can handle this situation delicately is to call a break, and then privately speak with the leader of the other team about your concerns.

Work on keeping the meeting moving in the right direction through positive language. Sharpen your listening skills during negotiations. This is vital. You are looking for both verbal and non-verbal cues that give you more information about how the opposition is thinking and feeling. Watch for non-verbal cues that give away the other party's emotions. Here are a few things to look for:

- Crossing arms and legs might be a giveaway for defensiveness or lack of agreement
- If you see fidgeting, small gestures and movements shifting their body away from you, it could signal a lack of agreement
- Leaning back in the chair and slightly holding their head down could indicate boredom
- Raising eyebrows and widening eyes might be an indication of surprise or questioning
- Tapping fingers or feet, frowning, getting out of their chair and pacing could be a sign of frustration or impatience

Different colours will demonstrate different behaviours when they are frustrated or stressed. Each of the colours could do the following:
1. Reds might become aggressive, demonstrative and threatening

2. Yellows might become very talkative, stop listening or jump from topic to topic, then impulsively agree
3. Greens might acquiesce (i.e. give in), nod frequently, appearing to be in agreement while deep down they don't agree
4. Blues might begin to ask for more and more details and get stuck in analysis paralysis

Maintain subconscious rapport by mirror and matching body language and tonality, even if you see these stonewalling behaviours. At the first opportunity, assertively ask for a break: *"It seems like a good time for a break so we can regroup our thoughts."* If you are dealing with multiple people, during the break try to lobby with a sympathetic person from the other side or someone with whom you have established strong rapport. Ask them to help bring everyone on their team back to focusing on moving things forward. Review the chapter on Conversational Self-defense to pick up tools that can help you to shift the negotiation back on track.

Observe the opposition closely, looking for inconsistencies in their behaviour. If you see someone pretending they don't care about reaching an agreement or appearing reluctant to provide solutions, you need to re-stress the need for agreement and remind them of how far you have come by repeating all the points in common. Maintain direct eye contact and a positive tone. Let them know that you have continued to be flexible throughout the process and you want to work toward a mutually-beneficial result for all parties.

If the opposition gives you an ultimatum, insults you or makes threats, calmly let them know that you will stop all negotiations until they are ready to work with you constructively. Then re-affirm the common ground and restate the key objectives to get them focused on the issues.

You might also meet those who will attempt to manipulate you by trying to break you down with emotional appeals that may or may not be valid. This is the time to let them know that you want things to work our fairly for everyone, then move the conversation back to the business at hand. You might have to restate the objectives or review portions of the proposal where you have already made a compromise.

Step 7: Move to a closing

As you move through the negotiation agenda, there will be a number of agreements and disagreements along the way. Track every decision and agreement in writing exactly as it is stated so that everyone can see and review them at any time.

Pushing for a close can be a delicate process. You certainly won't want to try to close things too quickly. Can you live with the ambiguity of not knowing exactly what the deal with end up looking like? You need to have enough patience and resilience to outlast the opposition. I have seen many people get worn down, become impulsive and agree too quickly because they run out of patience and are too eager to wait for the right deal. At the same time, don't just stall for dramatic effect; find the correct balance between momentum and stalling.

Shift your body language when you are about to make the actual final proposal. Lean forward, sit upright in your chair and make direct eye contact – this will subconsciously send the signal that you are attentive and serious about finalizing the deal.

I once witnessed a young man lean back in his seat, throw his arm over the back his chair and stretch his legs out just before he was about to present the final fee for a project. I immediately noticed Henry, the customer, raise his eyebrows and begin to frown. I was there on behalf of Henry to help him choose the right supplier for a project. Up until this moment things seemed to be going very well, but now the customer was turned off. The young man mentioned the price with a big grin on his face. Henry appeared very annoyed, got up abruptly and said to the young man, "We will get back to you" before leaving the room. I said goodbye to the supplier, then went to meet with Henry.

I asked him what happened. Henry said, "You know, at first he seemed serious about getting my business, but did you see how he just got all relaxed at the end, as if he expected he was going to get the deal? He was inconsistent and arrogant. I know I won't work will with a guy like that." Henry had made up his mind and wouldn't budge on his decision. I was surprised how quickly the young man lost the deal because of his body language.

You could use a **hypothetical close**. Start by saying something like, "How would you feel if we settled on 20%?" then wait to see the person's response. This gives you the opportunity to test the waters, so to speak. You can probe for their emotional reaction. A hypothetical close helps everyone to save face because it is not definite and can be taken off the table if you receive a negative response.

Here are a few additional examples of hypothetical closes:
- If we reduce the price by an additional 15%, will you agree that we are your exclusive supplier?

- If we were able to pay for your certification program, would you agree to the 10% raise?
- If we increase your rate by $100 per hour, will you take on this additional project?

Recently I decided to purchase a leather chair at a local furniture store. I arrived at 8:45 pm, fifteen minutes before closing, and began to wander around the store. I came upon a leather chair I really liked and the best news was, it had a discount tag. As I examined it, a salesperson approached me. I told him I was interested in a few items, including the discounted chair.

One by one he went over the specifications for each item, until we got to the chair I wanted. The salesperson began to go over the features and functions, and I asked him why it was discounted. He said that it had been on the showroom floor for a while due to it being part of a previous line. *Bingo!* I had heard enough. I now knew that the store was very motivated to get this chair sold because they needed to free up space in the showroom.

I made up my mind to negotiate for that leather chair and opened by telling him that I was interested in the discounted chair, but it cost more than the budget I had in mind. "What budget do you have in mind?" he asked. "Well, I'm not willing to pay this much for sure," I responded. "Please tell me your best offer."

He discounted it by an additional $100 dollars, plus threw in a leather care kit (valued at $100). His response gave me an idea of his potential discount threshold; he was willing to give up $200 worth of value. The fact is that the $100 kit probably only cost the store $10, but putting a higher value to it gave it a greater perceived value.

So I tried a hypothetical close by asking him, "Would you be willing to extend the discount to $200, instead of providing the leather care kit which I don't really need?" After a bit of pacing back and forth, he agreed. I was also able to negotiate $25 off the $75 delivery cost. It was good news for everyone. I got a great deal – a $1500 leather chair for $350, and the store had a free spot to place a new piece.

Another closing tactic is a **conditional offer**, where you propose a set of conditions for each party in order for the deal to move forward. For instance you might say, "If you do X, then we will do Y." This gives you a way to gauge which conditions or options might be suitable to the other party.

In addition to working on conditional and hypothetical closes, you will probably make a few **concessions** along the way. A concession is a trade-off where you give up or concede to part of your proposal in order to keep the negotiations moving. Whenever you make a compromise, you want to ensure that you are trading something in your proposal for a concession from the other party.

Never go into negotiations with just one main position or demand because this doesn't give you any room to maneuver. Think of your final proposal as a package or bundle with various component pieces that make up the whole. If you don't get the salary increase you are looking for, what else would be a suitable substitute? You should have already thought through all the desirable options before making concessions along the way. Start by making small concessions at first, because sometimes agreements can be reached sooner than you think. People want different things and often an agreement is reached because you are not competing for the same thing.

When everything has been agreed upon, you need to secure all the details with a full write-up of the deal. The paperwork should include information about the terms and conditions, method and schedule of payment, dates, times and milestones and so on. Always thank the other party for working with you in conducting a successful negotiation, and follow through with all the promises that you made during the deal.

Finally, keep in mind the long-term health of the relationship for all the people involved. Think about the long-term benefits when you negotiate, not just short-term gain. My litmus test for a great negotiation is for everyone to have met their key objectives and still respect each other in the morning.

EXERCISE

Practice your new negotiation skills by using the questions below to plan a strategy to negotiate a salary increase with your manager and any other relevant party(s).

What are your objectives? Describe your process of preparing, planning, brainstorming options, presenting and closing the deal.

1. Why is this negotiation necessary? (Discuss purpose and objectives)

2. How do you prepare the materials? What would you prepare before the session? What are your sources for research?

3. Who will attend the session? Assess the opposition – for each attendee, identify what you think might be their initial position in reference to the potential

outcome (e.g. very supportive, unsure, undisclosed, openly opposed, etc.)

4. How would you begin the session?

5. Which alternatives will you introduce if you don't get agreement to your first option?

6. What conclusions do you anticipate?

7. How do you think you will feel throughout the process?

CHAPTER FOURTEEN

Essential Interview Skills and Techniques

One of the most important places to use your newly-developed chameleon communication skills is in an interview. What do you think about when you hear the word "interview." This is an interesting process because people will list words and phrases such as: nervous, anxious, competition, confidence, and being judged.

To be an excellent candidate, there are a variety of things you need to do to be thoroughly prepared and position yourself as a top choice. These include the activities you need to do *before the interview*, *during the interview* and *after the interview*. The most central aspect to being a strong interviewee is to be prepared.

Before The Interview – Preparation Stage

The emotion most often associated with interviews is nervousness. The greatest remedy for that is, you guessed it, to prepare. Preparation is the number one way to reduce this anxiety. Whenever I do career coaching, I instruct clients to:
- prepare the mind
- prepare the paper
- prepare the look
- prepare for questions

You can significantly reduce the butterflies in your stomach when you build your confidence through adequate preparation.

Prepare the Mind

The first essential thing you need in order to create an effective interview experience is to *prepare yourself mentally*. Having negative thoughts will not help you to make the right impression, nor project to anybody that you are a confident person. You mind will trigger anxiety if you are thinking about the competition and asking yourself if you are suitable, or if you will make the right impression. Examine your assumptions, thoughts and emotions when you envision yourself in the interview. Do you appear credible?

Instead of thinking about the worst things that might happen, which will only increase your nervousness, you need to visualize yourself sitting confidently, upright in the chair in front of the interviewer. See yourself and the interviewer smiling and getting along well. Notice what a great job you are doing in responding to all his/her questions, while the interviewer appears very receptive as you discuss your expertise and qualifications.

Take this visualization even further. See, hear and feel what it is like to actually receive the phone call, when you get the great news that you were their top choice. What would you do? Would you jump around howling *Yippee!* or sit quietly and allow the news to sink in? Live the moment as if it were already true. Affirm to yourself that you are the best person for the job and there's no reason why you shouldn't get it.

Once in a while someone will ask me if visualizations and affirmations really work. My answer is always *"Yes, if you do it right."* **Visualizations** and

affirmations form the basis of preparing you mentally, emotionally and physically to perform the task. This means that if you are visualizing or affirming, you need to involve the mind, the body and your feelings. Specifically, **visualization** is a mental technique that builds mental imagery to which your emotions and body responds. It will allow you to sit on your sofa and literally sense the situation as if it were real.

Visualizations have been used by athletes for many years to enhance their performance. One of the most popular studies on the power of visualizations was carried out by Russian scientists on a group of Olympic athletes. In 1980, the work of these scientists became public. Russian coaches and sport psychologists had been utilizing mental imagery training for years with their athletes, who would mentally rehearse, repeating their routines over and over in their mind hundreds of time prior to a competition. For the study, scientists broke the athletes into four groups, who did varying levels of visualization and physical training. The mental training was designed for athletes to focus on improving their performance in their sport.

The four groups were made up as follows:
- Group 1 did 100% physical training and no mental training at all
- Group 2 did 75% physical training with 25% mental training
- Group 3 did 50% physical training and 50% mental training
- Group 4 did 25% physical training and with the most mental training, 75%

The athletes then attended the 1980 Winter Olympics in Lake Placid. After tabulating the final results, the scientists reported that group 4 had the most improvement of all the groups. Yes, the athletes who did the most visualization and the least physical training. Even more surprising was that group 1, who did no mental training but practiced constantly, improved the least. Group 3 also did better than group 2, thereby showing how powerful mental rehearsal can be in producing lasting changes in human behaviour.

In another study by Australian psychologist and educator Alan Richardson, he demonstrated how basketball players improved the number of successful free-throws with both daily visualization and physical practice. In this 20-day study, there were three groups of basketball players whose routines varied as follows:
1. Group A *physically* practiced shooting free-throws for 20 minutes for the 20 days and improved their performance by 24%
2. Group B *mentally* practiced shooting free-throws for 20 minutes for the 20 days and improved their performance by 23%
3. Group C had no practice at all and showed no improvement

This study illustrates that physical practice and mental practice provide almost the same level of result in performance improvement. I offer you this evidence of the usefulness of mental practice in the hope that you will at least try visualizing your success the next time you have an interview, an important meeting, or any event where you would like to enhance your chance of succeeding. Visualizing does not replace the need for practical preparation on a physical level, however, but as research has shown, it can give you that extra edge that might make all the difference.

There are many theories of how mental imagery might affect the body. One of the ideas I have found interesting is the concept of the **ideomotor** effect. This term refers to the automatic muscular reflex response that occurs due to a thought. Under hypnosis I may prompt a client to indicate a "yes" or "no" response with a specific finger, or even to raise a hand if they feel any discomfort. These are called hypnotic suggestions, which I carry out prior to fully inducing the client into hypnosis. These ideomotor responses have worked very effectively even when the client is in a deep trance, and they are not consciously controlling their finger or hand.

I often demonstrate a simple ideomotor sensory response by asking my students to imagine biting on a lemon, which usually produces salivation. Essentially, the mental thought affects the body to produce the physical response. Therefore as you are visualizing your success, the mind is affecting the body to reduce the nervous symptoms that might be produced due to thoughts of failure.

Earlier in the book I discussed the example of a client who had negative thoughts about her job every Sunday evening, with the end result being frequent anxiety and panic attacks. Think about it – if negative thoughts can cause us anxiety, then positive thoughts and mental imagery can elicit positive feelings. When you attend an interview, these great feelings will give you that extra edge you need to walk in with confidence.

The second part of preparing the mind is to gather business intelligence to develop a solid understanding of the company and the specific people you will encounter at your interview. You must *analyze the organization* – what are its vision, mission, values, and goals? These will help you to determine their level of progressiveness and get a glimpse of their corporate culture.

Employers are always looking for a candidate who will have the correct balance between qualification and a good cultural fit. You need to decide if the company will be a good fit for you as well. What do you know about its products, services and delivery methodologies? These will help you to determine if the nature of the work will suit you.

Researching an organization is easier than it has ever been in history. The Internet and all its services – websites, wikis, blogs and social networks – are all tremendous resources for digging up useful information about your prospect company and its staff.

Do the leg work to learn as much as you can about the company. Publically-traded companies, government bodies and most not-for-profit organizations will have annual reports and other such company briefing documents. Ask for the names of the individuals who will be interviewing you. Now look them up on current and popular social networking sites. You may find that you share mutual interests, a common academic background, or you're both from the same hometown.

Don't shortcut this research process. If researching your future employers makes you feel uncomfortable, think again. Your competition is probably doing it, so why not arm yourself with all the information you may need leading up to that meeting? It might be a cliché, but knowledge is power. Even if you don't use it in an interview, the things you know will make you feel prepared and powerful.

Pre-Employment Assessment

Many organizations today require their shortlisted applicants to complete a pre-employment assessment test. These tests are used as part of the selection criteria to find the best match and narrow down the number of candidates who might be suitable for the job. These types of tests can be IQ and EQ tests, personality tests, background checks, reference checks and police checks. I am frequently asked if these tests are legal and the simple answer is yes. Companies have a right to verify candidates for employment as long as the tests are administered by a professional and are non-discriminatory based upon the Human Rights Code.

Early in my career I wanted to find out what one of these reports might say about me. Thus, I hired a company who administered assessments and I completed a number of these tests. It was a very enlightening experience to have the reports debriefed to me as if I were about to hire myself. I now knew how a candidate like myself would be positioned for an employer. It was well worth the investment, because I became much better at describing my abilities in the language that employers wanted to hear.

It is important that you become comfortable with assessments, so that you too can gain a better understanding of your attributes and skills. If you have never done one, I encourage you to take a standardized assessment to enhance your understanding of yourself, thereby giving you a powerful way to talk about your qualifications with a prospective employer.

Part of the services I offer is to work with individuals and companies to conduct pre-employment testing utilizing a standardized and validated reporting system that describes the individual's core competencies, behaviours and motivations, communication and leadership preferences and emotional intelligence. We also work with companies to produce Job Benchmarks which describe the competencies, behaviours and skills required for a specific job, so that we can match the candidates directly to the role.

Prepare the Paper

Preparing the paper includes the creation of your resume, gathering a list of references, and producing a portfolio of your key accomplishments, competencies and experiences.

Creating an effective **resume** is a vital part of any job hunt. There are basically three formats that are used for most resumes. These include the chronological format, the functional format, or a combination of the two.

A **chronological** style lists your work experience in reverse chronological format, with the most recent job listed first in the experience section and working backwards. This format is most advantageous for people who have a very specific career sector or subject matter experience. Many recruiters are comfortable and familiar with this format. A disadvantage of the chronological resume is that it will show gaps in your work history that you might have to explain to the interviewer. A second disadvantage of this format is that your experience need to match the criteria of skills needed for the potential job.

The more uncommon **functional** style, lists your work experience in specific skill clusters in order to focus attention on different areas of expertise. Dates and places of employment are left out, which could cause a lot of questions, but for certain positions this might be good because it highlights your marketable knowledge, experience and professional development. With this type of resume, you need to anticipate questions and be prepared to discuss the specific companies where you have worked.

The **combination** of functional and chronological gives you the best of both styles. You have the section for skills and achievements to focus attention on your competencies, and then you have the list of companies and dates. The only drawback of this format is the possibility that it might have too much information for a quick glance. The layout of the combination resume is very important. I recommend putting the skills and achievements in a box at the top of the resume after your name and contact information, and then add the chronological information.

Always bring a few copies of your resume to the interview, even if you have faxed or emailed it ahead. I have seen resumes that have been printed by the interviewer on scrap paper. You certainly wouldn't want your resume to be reviewed on scrap paper. I bring copies of the resume on nice textured paper so this will appeal to the different learning styles. This is great for the visuals (it looks nice) and the tactile interviewers (it feels great).

At a recent proposal meeting, I brought extra copies of my proposal printed on a bright white linen stock and placed in blue/gold linen portfolio covers. I handed a copy of the proposal to the key decision maker and he immediately ran his hands across the face of the folder and exclaimed, "Wow, this proposal already feels great." This was a great start to the meeting.

In regards to references, you should contact all your references ahead of the interview to request their help. I send all my references a briefing of the role or project I am applying for, along with key points for emphasis if they get a call.

A company hired me a few years ago to assist with a recruitment process for hiring a CFO. We were down to our last three candidates, whom we asked for references at the end of each interview. One individual had the list with him, which score him bit points with the executive director who put him at the top of the list. The second person hesitated when asked for references; this was a red flag and he was put to the end of the list. The third person said that she would send it as soon as she got home. It was interesting how the panel seemed to focus on the fact that the person who brought the reference list seemed organized and to be the best candidate. An interesting fact to note is that the executive director had a high Dominance factor (Red) and he really did not want to waste time chasing people for their reference lists.

I recommend that you arrive at every interview with a pre-prepared reference list that you can offer right on the spot. Also make sure to prepare your cover letters, follow-up letters, and thank-you letters ahead of time so that you can respond quickly and follow up on each interview in a timely manner.

Accomplishment Portfolio

The final part of preparing the paper is to keep a list of major projects where you have reflected on:
1. tangible results
2. key competencies you utilized or learned in doing the project
3. specialized training that you received
4. the overall impact or benefit of the project on the organization

For the companies that you have worked for, it is a good idea to demonstrate how your work has aligned with the larger organizational objectives. Use action-oriented words when you describe your accomplishments. Emphasize where you have solved problems, and any unique aspects of the solution(s) you created. Did you resolve any interpersonal/people problems? Did you save money? Did you increase or decrease something important? Did you have an effect on the quality of the service?

Wherever possible, you should use words that illustrate measurements; some of these include *quantity*, *percentages*, or *key statistics*. I call this the **Accomplishment Portfolio**, which you should update yearly by doing an inventory of key achievements so as to remind yourself of your growing marketability.

Describe your expertise in terms of competencies, not just skills. Employers have recognized that skills can be taught through one-day seminars, but competencies (which are typically innate) need to be developed over a longer period of time through actual experience, mentoring or coaching.

Are you aware of *your* core competencies? Based upon work I have done in the field, the following is a list of the most sought-after core competencies (note that competencies generally depend on the industry's particular needs):

- communication & interpersonal skills
- self-management
- personal accountability
- self-starter
- diplomatic/tactful
- leadership skills
- decision making
- problem solving
- analytical thinking

Prepare the Look

Your attire and accessories need to match the culture of the organization. Dress code is a chief factor in building rapport. You need to pay particular attention to what you select to wear.

I recall a meeting with a prospective client for a team building project. My research told me that this adventure travel company was very casual, and most of the pictures I saw online of the employees showed that they were primarily wearing jeans and T-shirts. I picked an outfit that was business casual – dressy jeans, high quality golf shirt, a jacket, black leather running shoes and a brown vintage messenger bag – for my meeting.

Sitting in the reception area of the company, I noticed a man arrive a few minutes later. He was wearing a blue two-piece suit, starched white shirt and red tie (the typical power suit, which might have been very affective in another setting). For a moment I thought, "Did I make the wrong read about this company?" The answer came quickly when the two gentlemen we were about to meet entered the reception area. Both were wearing blue jeans, white T-shirts and sneakers. Whew! I was relieved.

I was the first to interview with the executives of the company. Before I sat down, I removed my jacket and eased back in my chair, mirroring what they had done. A couple of minutes into the conversation, they began joking with me about how they could gently break it to the guy in reception that he was not going to be a good fit for their team building exercise. "He totally doesn't seem to get what we're all about", one of them said. They had formed this impression about my competitor in a few seconds. You can see how dressing incorrectly can really backfire.

The next scenario will demonstrate how wearing the wrong accessory can also create the wrong impression. A few years ago I worked with a not-for-profit organization to profile a short list of four candidates for a senior executive role. Once the profiles were complete, we set up a series of interviews to meet with each candidate. Everything was routine for the first couple of candidates, until the third person arrived. He entered the boardroom flashing an alligator skin briefcase, a Rolex watch and an Armani suit, and before long he was reviewing his big salary expectations. We were all a bit shocked since we had made it clear in the posting that the role was for a not-for-profit start-up, and had an expectation that the new hire would be assisting the organization with fund-raising. His qualifications were great, but he was not considered a good cultural fit. Again we see that having a mismatch between attire / accessories and culture can make the wrong impression.

Do your research about the company culture so you can determine the appropriate dress. Are you meeting on casual Friday? I recommend that you dress one level above the dress code for the culture of the organization (i.e. dress closer to formal than informal).

Prepare for Questions

An interviewer meets with potential employees in order to evaluate their skills, experience and qualification. In a structured meeting the interviewers will prepare a list of questions to guide the interview process. As a prospective employee, you need to be prepared to answer these questions efficiently and effectively. There are no standard responses for questions, but practice will help you to give answers that are relevant, accurate and impactful.

Many people feel uncomfortable and awkward when there is silence, so they try to fill the time with random small talk that may not have anything to do with the conversation or the question they are being asked. For that reason, when you respond to questions don't be afraid to take a silent moment to gather your thoughts before giving your response. Slow down your speed of speech a bit, unless you already speak very slowly – in which case you should try to speed up. Remember, you need to build rapport and flex to the DISC style and representational system of the person whom you are meeting.

Behavioural interviews

Behavioural style interviews have become very prevalent over the past 10 years. The theory behind behavioural interviewing is that the most accurate predictor of future performance is based upon how the person performed in the past, in a similar situation. In this type of interview, the interviewer describes a real on-the-job scenario and gauges if your answer demonstrates that you have the right experience in performing the relevant tasks.

Responses to behavioural interview questions must include real examples and the exact results. Earlier in this chapter we talked about the ***Accomplishment Portfolio***. Creating this portfolio will help you to prepare for behavioural questions. You will learn more about yourself, your past successes, what you had learned and how you have grown; by the end of it you will have an arsenal of concrete and specific examples of your accomplishments. You cannot and should not try to fake a behavioural interview, because the interviewer may ask you more specific questions about your example, explicitly things like, "What were you thinking when you discussed that with such and such?"

The more details you have about the job, the better you can prepare. However, most job postings don't give enough detail. Try to get a copy of the job description or job briefing before the interview. How? Just ask for it when your interview has been confirmed. If you cannot get it, carry out an Internet search for a sample job description (if you don't have one from your present job).

Once you have a job description, comb through it and write down the core responsibilities or key accountabilities, and then brainstorm the core competencies, skills, experiences and behaviours that would be required to perform well in the role. How well do *you* match up?

What the Interviewer Wants

No one is perfect and the interviewer doesn't expect you to be perfect, so your responses should not portray you as not having any failings or being impervious to making mistakes. Your honesty and sincerity will help your prospective employer to see the real you – your strengths and your progress. When I talk about how I grew to be more detail-oriented, I usually include a depiction of the circumstances of how I discovered this about myself, and how I developed processes and accommodations to improve my skills in this area. Interviewers want to see that you have a strong level of self-awareness, and that you are able, resourceful and self-motivated to seek out new ways to learn.

Review the following tips to prepare to do well on behavioural-based questions:

- Provide a brief description of the problem, challenge or situation
- Tell them what your action was & how you decided on that particular course of action
- Give a brief description of the result of your action, and your assessment of that result

Sample behavioural questions

Wouldn't it be great to have all the interview questions ahead of time? Although this is not possible, if you have experience and subject matter expertise, you can predict many of the questions based upon the type of role. These behavioural questions are *job-specific* and relate to specific tasks and activities for the role. An example was a question that I asked a potential financial officer – how he would handle a situation where each department had created budgets that exceeded the overall organizational financial resources.

You may be asked *competency-based* behavioural questions. These are designed to figure out your aptitude in various job competencies. Examples of these types of questions can be:

- Can you tell me about a time when you demonstrated initiative?
- Can you tell me about a challenging professional interpersonal situation and how you dealt with it?
- Can you tell me about one of your most difficult decisions – how did you make it and what was the outcome?
- Can you tell me about an experience in which you had to speak up and tell other people how you really felt?

Some of the toughest questions you don't want to be asked...

Every interviewee I have had the pleasure to counsel has told me about the questions they didn't like being asked. I have made a list of these questions so you can anticipate how you would respond.

Review the questions below and practice your responses to become comfortable with providing great answers:

1. What was the toughest decision you ever had to make?
2. Why do you want to work for this organization?
3. Why should we employ you?
4. If we hire you, what changes would you make?
5. What are your greatest strengths?
6. What are your greatest weaknesses?
7. Where do you see yourself in 5 years?
8. What are your salary expectations?
9. Tell me something about yourself?
10. Do you have any questions about the organization or the job?
11. What didn't you like about your previous job?
12. Are there any weaknesses in your education or experience?

Plan questions for the interviewer
If the interviewer asks you if you have any questions, never say no! Prospective employers expect that you will have questions to clarify the role and job conditions if you are truly interested in the position. These might be general questions about the company and its goals, about the people you will be working with (or for), and specifics about the job itself. You should definitely be asking about the next steps after the interview if this has not already been outlined for you.

As you will see in the upcoming example, my question to a potential employer about his strategic goals expressed my genuine interest and helped me to see how I could assist with these goals. This became the basis of a wonderful conversation about possibilities that took us both beyond the interview and into the future!

During the Interview

Back when I attended university, I had been commuting to classes for a couple of years and had grown tired of being on the road. When I decided to get a part-time job, my main criteria was to find somewhere close to home. I browsed the community paper and noticed that a local printing company was looking for a manager. I was thrilled, since it was just a 15 minute drive from home. I really wanted to get this job!

I did a bit of research beforehand and found out that the owner was a top sales executive who recently left his job to open this company. A lucky coincidence was that he used to work for the sister company of my last temporary workplace. I leveraged this fact in my resume, as well as noting my desire to work with a progressive entrepreneur. Once the resume was polished, I sent it in. A few days later, I got a call to come in for an interview.

On the day of the interview I arrived early to get familiarized with the setting. I sat in the waiting room with a couple of other candidates and overheard that both had extensive experience in the printing business. Fed up of listening to them try to outdo each other's credentials, I got up and wandered over to a guy sitting at a big computer screen. I introduced myself and he told me his name.

This was coincidence number two – it turns out that he had the exact first and last name of my best friend growing up. The difference was, my friend was a girl. He used Chris for Christopher and she used Chris for Christine. When I told him this, he laughed and said, "Looks like we are destined to be friends too."

I asked him about his work. He told me all about laser-graphics and how it was a method of making paper plates instead of metal plates. I finally broke down and told him that I had zero knowledge about the printing business, but I was eager to learn and would he teach me all about it when I got the job. He chuckled, "For sure I will, no problem, I'll show you everything I know."

While we were chatting a man approached us and said hello. Chris turned to him and said, "Hey Bob, meet my new friend Claudia. Claudia, this is Bob, the owner of our company."

We shook hands, "I'm here for the interview, I'm up in half an hour," I told him.

"I was just going to grab a sandwich but you can join me now if you want," said Bob.

We walked to the back of the building where there were a few offices in a row. I followed Bob to his desk and sat across from him. He said, "Let me take a look at your resume before we start."

I decided to save him the trouble. "I'll save you the time of reading my resume because I have no experience in the printing business."

Bob raised his eyebrows. "I see."

Fast forward, I explained to Bob that even though I did not have experience, I was an entrepreneurial spirit like him and really wanted to be part of building something. We both wanted similar things and if he could explain his goals for the business, I already had a few ideas on how he could begin to meet those objectives. Bob went over his business goals, explaining how he wanted to be the number one franchise within a year. I told him about a couple of ideas that came to mind while I was chatting with Chris, and he looked impressed with these ideas.

Finally, I told him that I was going to make it easy for him to say yes! Chris had volunteered to train me in the evenings so Bob could hire me for a couple of weeks at no charge, during which time I would come in to learn. In the meantime, he could still look for a backup candidate. Bob smiled, "I like how you think – okay, we have a deal."

I pushed my luck a little further and made a request to be paid a few thousand more than Bob originally intended, on the agreement that I would help him become number one sooner than a year. Moral of the story – I got the job and eight months later we were number one.

What do you notice about my interview with Bob? First, Bob and I had a conversation. Great interviews are great conversations. If you reframe interviews as conversations, it goes a long way to boost confidence and reduce anxiety. Secondly, I used several angles to build rapport. Finally, I provided an easy way for Bob to say yes by expressing my confidence in both myself and our ability to work together to actualize the company goals. Don't be afraid to have visionary thinking and share it with the interviewer. Figure out what his/her definition of success is and align yourself with it.

Making that great first impression

It takes only a few seconds to make a great first impression. A person forms their initial opinion of you based upon your appearance, attire, mannerisms, posture and your body language. To create a great first impression, your body language must demonstrate confidence and credibility. Consequently, remember to walk in with an upright posture and hold your head up high.

You need to exude an air of confidence that is perceived the minute you enter the room for your interview. Your first encounter is extremely important because it sets the tone for the meeting. In my experience, people have a bias for individuals who appear confident and self-assured more than for those who have lots of experience but cannot express themselves.

Two other vital pieces of non-verbal communication that you must perform well are the handshake and the smile. Your handshake must be firm and deliberate (careful not to squeeze too hard). Your smile must be a genuine, full body smile: your face, your eyes and your whole body must be beaming. Have an open stance with your arms at your side when standing, or on the table when seated. Crossing your arms might convey that you are bored or closed, so avoid this gesture.

Build subconscious rapport the instant you meet the interviewer by matching gestures and facial expressions. As the interview gets going, try matching their breathing pattern. Also, your verbal and non-verbal language must be aligned to convey a sense of believability and trustworthiness. *Refer to the chapter on building instant rapport and the importance of non-verbal language to learn more about these techniques.*

Treat everyone you meet with professionalism. This means receptionist, janitors and interviewers, and even other candidates. You can't know who might have an impact on the final decision. Years ago I was waiting in the lobby for a project interview. I noticed another consultant being very aggressive with the receptionist. He had arrived late and expected her to hurry off the phone so he could go up for the meeting. I found out later, after I won the project, that the receptionist was married to the owner. I asked her about the incident and she told me that she immediately called her husband and told him that the guy was belligerent and would not be a suitable for helping them to "improve corporate communication."

During an interview, you must watch for and avoid any idiosyncratic non-verbal habits – nail-biting, hair-twisting, drumming your finger on a desk, tapping your toes, chewing gum – these are all signs of nervousness. These aren't the only obvious distractions you might encounter –mobile phones that ring or vibrate during the interview must be turned off. You want the interviewer to focus totally on you and your responses, not on distracting body language and electronic interruptions.

Remember to reframe the interview into a conversation. Show enthusiasm when you're asking or responding to questions. In the example of my interview with Bob, I illustrated how to turn it into a conversation by asking relevant questions about the company. When the interviewer is asking questions or making a statement, do not interrupt. Allow them complete their sentence. Even if you think you know exactly what they are going to say, you might jump to the wrong conclusion and come across as presumptuous.

You truly need to use your active listening skills to clearly understand the question. Take your time when you answer, and respond succinctly. Remember that you should be flexing to the person's DISC Communication Style. You need to strike a balance by giving just the right amount of information, not too little for a Blue or Green interviewer and not too much for a Red or Yellow interviewer.

After the Interview

I advise you to make notes during the interview in order to keep track of key details or questions where you might want to provide further information. After the interview is over, your follow-up should take place within

48 hours, unless you have been asked not to correspond with the potential employer. Go out and buy yourself a few high quality thank you cards. I know this seems a bit old fashioned, but going retro with a card will help you stand out. Just think about how many emails the interviewer might be receiving versus how many real cards they may receive in the mail. You want to find ways to differentiate yourself from the herd.

Don't nag the interviewer. Avoid calling them back too soon, especially if they made it clear they were not open to receiving calls. It is entirely acceptable, however, for you to ask when they will be getting back to you, and you can ask permission to send an email with questions if you need further clarification. If another candidate happens to be chosen, still send a follow-up thank you letter, note or card, but not email.

You should prepare all your follow-up letters, cards and documents ahead of time so that your follow-up activities are not held up with trying to put documents together at the last minute.

Here's a list of items you might want to work on ahead of time:

- thank you cards and letter of acceptance
- inquiry emails about information
- request for time extension if you are given an offer and are not ready to accept

CHAPTER FIFTEEN

Masterful Meetings

Meetings are one of the primary instruments for conducting business. A recent study revealed that there are approximately 11 million meetings in the United States every day. If we take just 10% of this number, we can say that there are over 1 million meetings taking place in Canada each day. These statistics are staggering when we combine this data with another statistic, which surveyed 1000 executives and found that they spend, on average, 17 hours per week in meetings, and reported that one-third of that time is wasted. This translates into over 5 hours wasted each week on ineffective meetings. If companies could improve how they conducted meetings, they would gain a tremendous increase in their productivity.

So what could be some of the reasons behind meetings not working as they should? In his book *Achieving Effective Meetings – Not Easy But Possible*, Bradford D. Smart cited a survey of 635 executives who reported on the characteristics that represent ineffective meetings. The percentages in the table below are eye-opening.

Characteristic	Percentage Reported
Drift away from the subject	83%
Poor preparation	77%
Questionable effectiveness	74%

Lack of listening	68%
Verbose participants	62%
Too long	60%
Lack of participation	51%

How many times have *you* been in a meeting where someone dominated the conversation while many others just sat there saying nothing? What about those meetings where you arrive and there's no agenda, and everyone seems to be having their own sidebar conversation? How about when there are so many topic tangents that you can't keep things straight? If we don't get a handle on managing the issues that affect how well we run our meetings, a lot of time and productivity goes down the drain, and in the end, everybody suffers.

In 1993, GM Consultants of Pittsburgh conducted a study where they described what people are looking for in effective meetings. Their results are published in the following table:

Factor	Percentage Reported
Participation	88%
Define the meeting's purpose	66%
Address each item on the agenda	62%
Assign follow-up action	59%
Record discussion	47%
Invite essential personnel	46%
Publish an agenda	36%

Upon reviewing this list, you can see that Participation and Purpose top the list. The interesting thing is that when people know the purpose of a meeting, they find it a lot easier to participate. The stated purpose defines where they need to focus their preparation to readily be an active participant. If you think about it, it makes total sense that these two items would be at the top of the list of criteria people look for in meetings!

Effective meetings don't just happen. Even the smoothest, most inspired meetings call for careful preparation leading up to the date. An effective meeting requires deliberate and strategic planning to ensure that purpose, agendas and logistics are well thought-out. A vital ingredient is the presence of a strong leader who will conduct the meeting in an efficient manner. Finally, participants must be prepared to participate!

Around four years ago I developed an effective program to assist a CEO to improve the meetings in his organization. I needed to determine the core problems that created negative experiences in their meetings, so I pick one of the meetings for actively observation.

I was sent an email asking me to be present on a Thursday afternoon at 2:00pm at a well-known golf and country club. The setting was fantastic. We were in a boardroom with large picture windows overlooking a large portion of the golf course. On a table in front of the window there was a cocktail platter, bottles of wine, cold beer and several other beverages. There were eight department heads in the meeting, along with myself. We were instructed to help ourselves to refreshments, and everybody was happy to oblige.

I noticed we did not have an agenda, the meeting began with the CEO asking everyone if they had anything to report. In no apparent order, individuals began to talk about project tasks that were partially completed. As one person spoke it would then stimulate another participant to offer some new great idea about how to modify what was already done, and so on. Once in a while the CEO would jump in, asking, *What else should we be discussing?*

Everyone took their own notes. The meeting ran from 2:00pm to 6:00pm, at which point one of the senior officers exclaimed, *Hey we've been at this for a while, what do you say we wind things down for today?* At this time the CEO agreed and they ordered another round of drinks, wine and cheese, basically adjourning the meeting.

During the debrief with the CEO, I wanted to know if the purpose of the meeting was to brainstorm. The CEO said "Sort of, we meet to discuss how projects are going and then see what other great ideas come out of the discussion." My response was, "And how do you track what is complete and what else will be done, because I noticed that no one took minutes?" He reflected on my question and then said "They must be keeping track of their own department information. I have a very creative and innovative team. Really great minds, but it is hard getting them to focus on getting things done."

The answer can sometimes be more obvious to an outsider looking into a situation than to its regular participants. In our sessions, I helped the CEO understand why his team had not completed many components of their projects over a several year period. Out of his eight department heads, he had seven who all had Yellow DISC Communication profiles. This meant that they were all more interested in generating ideas and brainstorming than implementation. This resulted in **scope creep** – a circumstance where you go beyond initially agreed-upon project parameters. It was easy to see why he had so many Yellows – he hired people just like himself, ideas people – because these people impressed him most of all.

It took us a couple of weeks to review each project, creating project management documentation and freezing the scope so that developers had certainty about what they had to create. I also designed and deployed a twelve step guideline for planning and running all meetings in the company, which resulted in vast improvements.

Twelve Steps To More Effective Meetings

1. Only have a meeting if it is really necessary.
2. All meetings must have a clear objective or purpose.
3. Who should be involved in the meeting?
4. All meetings must have an agenda.
5. Assign and circulate relevant meeting information and reports prior to the meeting.
6. Meetings must start and end on time so as not to punish those who are punctual. This also sets the stage for how serious you are about making the meeting effective.
7. Meeting participants must be prepared to participate.
8. Meeting minutes (i.e. notes) must be recorded.
9. Meeting decisions must be documented.
10. Action items must be documented and followed up.
11. Have a strong chairperson or a neutral facilitator.
12. Review meeting effectiveness at the end.

Step 1: Only conduct a meeting if it's really necessary

Often meetings are held to provide information to the participants. There are so many other ways to share information without having to gather everyone in one room, but I know why people have project status meetings.

Even though individuals could read the information on their own, people insist on project meetings because we feel that others won't pay attention to our status updates unless we announce them face-to-face.

You can implement a sign-off policy to ensure people are reading the updates, (i.e. have personnel provide their initials to confirm that they've read status notes). One of my clients in the Developmental Services sector implemented a staff communications book where every shift change care-worker must indicate they have read the day's log by initializing the pages. The team leader does a periodic follow-up to test that the staff did actually read the logs. Put this kind of information in a central place so it is easily accessible by all stakeholders.

If you send email updates, you can also create a "read receipt" which will tell you if the person has opened your email. If you see that they haven't yet opened it, you can do a follow-up. Generally I will give the person a quick phone call to indicate that there is an important memo waiting for their review. This will take a lot less time than having a group meeting.

In addition, if you need to make a quick consultative decision, it can be done with a quick round of phone calls to individuals to get information and opinions so that you can reach a resolution on your own without the need to bring everyone together.

Step 2: All meetings must have a clear objective or purpose

Meetings must have a significant purpose in order to run well. Some of the purposes may include:
- Solving problems
- Group decision-making

- Sharing information
- Project status meetings
- Team building

To determine a meeting's purpose, you need to ask, "What is the end result we wish to achieve, or what accomplishment would make the time spent worthwhile?" If you are meeting to make a decision, make sure everyone knows that you will not be leaving until the decision is made. There will be times when you really need to assert your focus to keep on track to achieve the objectives.

> In the space below write down what are some of the reasons you have meetings? Any of the reasons listed above?

Once you have a clear purpose, ask yourself if you really need a meeting to accomplish this objective? If you find that you require the input of multiple people for decision making or problem solving, you probably need a meeting. Studies have shown that group decisions have a higher quality when compared to decisions made by individuals.

Step 3: Who should be involved in the meeting?

Once you have decided that there is a significant purpose for the meeting, ask yourself a few key questions in order to plan an effective session. Ask yourself, "Who really needs to be present at the meeting?"

I have attended numerous meetings where there were people attending who had nothing to contribute, while critical individuals were missing. Carefully think through – who needs to attend this meeting? Selecting the right people to participate will ensure that you make the most productive use of your time together.

You probably already know that participating in meetings is one of the most important ways you can get noticed for your expertise and experience. Group situations give you an opportunity to demonstrate leadership, initiative and your creativity. Meetings are among the best device to help you get seen by the right people.

Individuals who have interactions with senior executives in meetings may be granted special projects since they have a chance to network with people who could advance their career.

Working in cross-functional teams through meetings is also a great way to expose you to other areas of the company that may peak your interest. There will be meetings that are compulsory for you to attend, but you should find ways to become involved in meetings for a strategic reasons – participate in meetings that might further your career.

Last year, I had the pleasure of working with a very accomplished manager who had a great deal of difficulty getting any recognition for her work because her boss either took all the credit or passed the credit onto other departments.

We developed a strategy to move her past this unfair situation. She would advocate to be assigned to special projects where she could attend meetings and network with individuals who were senior people in her organization. The plan worked very well. As the year progressed, she began to receive acknowledgement for her team and herself for their many award-winning initiatives.

Step 4: All meetings must have an agenda.

In the example I gave earlier about the CEO, he confessed that he rarely had agendas for his meetings since he felt this would stifle the creative process. However, after I calculated how much meetings were costing him with very little return on the investment, he became a great fan of agendas. The meetings substantially improved once everyone began creating and using an agenda.

Agendas serve many functions in meetings. Agendas are an instrument to keep meetings on track, both in terms of timing and topics. A standard agenda should have at least the following items:
- a. Logistical information such as time (start time and end time), date and location of the meeting (separated at the top for ease of visibility)
- b. Topics for discussion (each numbered)
- c. A presenter for each topic
- d. Allotment of time for each topic

Agendas are an efficient meeting management tool, because when people begin to drift off topic you can point them back to the agenda by saying, "I think we have gone off topic." An agenda helps the chairperson to keep speakers within the pre-established time frames and ensure that the meeting runs on time. The chair also uses the agenda at the beginning to set the stage for the meeting and to reinforce and gain participant commitment to keep on track.

Meeting agendas also serve an important purpose for participants prior to the meeting. The meeting planner should solicit input on the agenda from other key participants to ensure important topics are not missed. Each participant should then receive a copy of the agenda at least one week to ten days in advance of the meeting. This means sure that everyone attending the meeting will be aware of what will be happening so that they can get adequately prepared.

Additionally, an attendee can determine from the agenda if they will be useful in the meeting, and decide if it really makes sense for them to go.

Finally, the agenda is useful for doing a recap of topics and action items at the end of the meeting.

Step 5: Assign and circulate relevant meeting information and reports prior to the meeting.

One of the most crippling ways to sabotage a meeting is by not providing relevant information or reports to participants ahead of time. I've seen many meetings where participants were handed a detailed report at the beginning of the meeting, with the expectation that we would read, analyze, and formulate comments in order to make a decision. This usually made it impossible or ineffective for participants to do justice to the task.

All information, reports, and previous meeting minutes should be distributed along with the agenda. Meeting information should include:

a. meeting objective or purpose
b. what the participants need to know before attending the meeting
c. meeting agenda location/date/time / AV Equipment / Whiteboard / Flipchart
d. background information, documentation and reports
e. assigned items to speakers for preparation

Step 6: Start and end meetings on time

How many times have you arrived for a meeting only to find the room empty? You wait for few minutes and when no one shows up you run back to your desk. Possibly you feel upset that you were the only one who took the start time seriously. Time is so valuable. It is imperative to express respect for all meeting participants by showing up on time.

Meetings must start and end on time so as not to punish those who are punctual. Starting promptly sets the stage for how serious you are about making the meeting effective. I always have the start and end time clearly printed at the top of the agenda to keep the time expectations visible.

Sometimes it is hard to change people's habits around start and stop times because it is part of the culture. I ran into this with a client whose boss often came late to the meeting. This held up everyone since they waited for her to arrive before starting. My client Cindy was getting quite upset because her team felt that they were wasting so much time waiting around for the meetings to start. This forced everyone to stay late after work to finish their tasks.

I recommended that Cindy approach her boss to talk about this problem. Cindy was very nervous because she felt it would be like she was reprimanding her boss, a career-limiting move. I told her that it's all in how you say it. We developed the following script for her manager:

"I want to talk about our project meetings. I feel badly because I have been asking the team to wait for your arrival before starting the meeting, and then we end up running overtime. The result is my staff has to stay after hours to make up the lost time. Would you mind if we begin

without you if you are delayed, and I can get you caught up through the minutes?"

Cindy's boss was surprised that Cindy had never brought this to her attention before. Turns out the boss thought the team used the time at the beginning for a bit of personal catch up, so it didn't matter if she was late. Cindy was happy because her boss agreed that the team should not wait for her arrival to begin meetings. It took a few of weeks to get everyone comfortable about starting on time, but eventually all were present on time for meetings, including Cindy's boss.

Electronic distractions

Modern meetings are plagued with distractions due to the use of an ever-expanding array of digital devices. We see people in meetings engage in texting, glancing at their laptops, while others leave the room to take phone calls simply because their mobile phone screen lit up. These individuals indicate that they are multitasking to make better use of the time, but you and I both know this does not work. And if you do it too much, you risk looking unprofessional to your colleagues. Meetings tend to last longer, and we have to repeat information when individuals re-enter the room. How can meetings be effective with these types of distractions?

I have heard of offices charging a fine for those who disrupt meetings in this way, making it mandatory for you to pay $2 every time you use your cell phone. In my opinion, it would be preferable to shorten the meeting with a focus on finishing the agenda without interruption and asking those who interrupt to leave. If a person leaves and re-enters the room just carry on. Do not stop to get them up to speed.

There may be a few exceptions where you really do need to take a call. If this is the case, you should announce this to the group at the beginning of the meeting, so that when the call comes in you can excuse yourself and leave the room without appearing rude or unprofessional.

Step 7: Meeting participants must be prepared to participate

As a meeting participant, your responsibility is to be prepared to participate. Think about your preparation as split into three stages:
1. Preparation before attending
2. Active engagement during the meeting
3. Follow-up after the meeting

Your first task in preparation for a meeting is to get the pre-work completed. If you have not received the agenda, minutes or meeting information, take it upon yourself to ask the meeting planner or chairperson for this information.

Review the agenda so that you can bring specific documents or reports that are needed to the meeting. Create any required report ASAP so that you have time to prepare how you will present it at the meeting.

Use the agenda to pre-frame your mind so that you understand the purpose and focus of the event. This will prevent tangents or streams of random talking during discussions. Review all agenda topics and prepare your thoughts. This will help you to consider what you might want to bring up in the meeting. Typically in the milieu of the meeting it is hard to remember all you might have intended to say. Therefore, you should jot down a checklist of all relevant information you wish to relay to the group.

Using these checklists of key points will be a useful tool to prevent you from missing or forgetting items that you wanted to share.

Frequently, meetings are called as a formality to roll-out decisions that are made well before the meeting even takes place. If you want to have any impact on these decisions, you need to lobby prior to the meeting to get a chance to have your opinions heard.

Lobbying is the act of attempting to influence decisions or advocating for specific interests through pre-meetings and private conversations. Some people feel that lobbying is an unfair practice because it allows for certain individuals to obtain a greater opportunity to influence how certain topics will proceed in a meeting. The reality is, lobbying is a strategic tool that ensures you have an opportunity to have input on subjects that affect you and others in your team. Do your lobbying.

Arrive early to meetings. If you're early, you will always be on time! Even if you are not the chair you should still use your knowledge of the meeting process to help it run smoothly. By understanding the twelve steps outlined here, you will play your part as an informal leader in modeling behaviours that you know will make the meeting better.

During the meeting, seize the opportunity to speak up when it is appropriate to share your expertise or experience on a topic area. Sometimes participants are nervous to speak up in a group for fear of looking bad or saying the wrong thing. You have to move past your fear, so take a deep breath and go ahead – make your statement in a constructive and concise manner.

A meeting participant can subtly support the chairperson to facilitate the meeting. As you express your leadership skills, your active participation will not go unnoticed. The chart below shows many of the ways that you can contribute to ensure a more effective meeting.

Constructive Participant Activity	How?
INITIATING ACTIVITY	New thinking / new process
BREAKING THE ICE & SET COMFORTABLE ATMOSPHERE	Close-ended questions and small talk
SEEKING INFORMATION / OPINIONS	Open-ended questions
GIVING INFORMATION / OPINIONS	Use clear concise language with emotional control
ELABORATING	Extend and expand on other participants' ideas
CO-ORDINATING	Link similar ideas / perspectives
REALITY CHECK	Ensure the outcome is achievable
DIAGNOSING	Find out what roadblocks exits
MEDIATING	Reconcile differences
RELIEVING TENSION	Diminish negative behaviours / feelings
ACTIVE LISTENING	Paraphrase for clarity and understanding
SUMMARIZING	Restate what you heard for confirmation
DIVERGENT THINKING	Brainstorm ideas without evaluating them
CONVERGENT THINKING	Summarize key points, decisions and action steps

These constructive activities will help to keep the discussion flowing in a meeting. Always diffuse arguments quickly if you notice tempers heating up. Use some of the following phrases to keep the momentum:

- *It seems like we have been going around in circles, maybe we should summarize what has been said.*
- *I know that this is a sensitive subject, but we really need to remain respectful to each other*
- *It appears that emotions are heating up; this might be a good time for a stretch break*
- *Can I suggest that we keep to the facts and not put each other down*

Before you leave the meeting, clarify what tasks you are responsible to complete, as well as set deadlines. After the meeting you will have to take personal accountability to complete action items, review minutes and help to follow up on various activities that were delegated during the meeting. I suggest that you start as soon as possible to get the tasks done so that you can deliver in the agreed-upon timelines.

Step 8: Meeting minutes must be recorded.

Minutes describe the events of the meeting, including a list of attendees, a statement of the issues discussed by the participants, and related responses or decisions on these issues. Writing a verbatim report is not a typical way to write minutes. You should write the minutes as a summary of the discussion and make sure to include decisions and action items.

Meeting minutes (i.e. meeting notes) must be recorded and made part of the company's meeting information archives. This archive needs to be stored on a centrally-available computer server so that anyone can refer to the minutes at any time. A formal or semi-formal set of minutes should be distributed to everyone who attended so they can verify the correctness of the information.

Increasingly, I've seen meetings where there is no designated note-taker to create a single set of comprehensive minutes. Instead, each individual is required to take their own meeting notes. This becomes problematic because people vary in how they take notes. Some people take no notes at all, some very little and others too much.

This is specifically challenging for two key reasons: 1) individuals are writing down their own interpretation of what has been said in the meeting, and 2) there are individuals who think they will remember everything and never write down the action items or commitments they make during the meeting.

I recommend that you solicit the group for a volunteer to take a notes that will become the official record of the meeting. Many groups take turns with the note-taking task, which is also a great way to build ownership among team members.

Step 9: Meeting decisions must be documented.

How many times have you left a meeting with an certain understanding of a decision, only to find out a few days later that everyone has a different memory about what was said? This is one of the most common causes of frustration among meeting attendees. They report that feeling as if others are trying to make up their own decisions rather than follow the group decision.

As you know by now, our minds distort information. So imagine what is happens during a group discussion where several people give their opinions on a subject and everyone is tracking the decisions in their own notes. It results in each participant walking away more or less hearing what they wanted to hear.

It is crucial that you record all the decisions made in the meeting, then reiterate them back to all the participants prior to closing the meeting. I suggest recording all decisions made on a separate sheet of paper that is kept aside to be used for quick reference or to be reviewed with the group.

Step 10: Action items must be documented and followed up.

You know that after an hour or two of discussions people end up walking away, worn out and probably already have forgotten some of the commitments they made in the meeting. Use the minutes to do the follow-up for action items.

There is a useful practice I've used with taking meeting notes which you may find helpful. I keep a separate colour sheet of paper to record action items and decisions. When it comes time to wrap up and summarize the meeting, I pull out this sheet of paper. This makes it easy for me to do a quick review of the commitments and decisions. Help people to remember what to do and reinforce their commitment.

The manager, chairperson, or an appropriate participant, must be appointed to follow-up on the completion of all action items.

Step 11: Have a strong chairperson or a neutral facilitator

Meeting facilitation is not an easy task, yet great improvements can be made by having meetings led by a highly effective chairperson. A great chairperson is a leader, a participant and a facilitator all at the same time. As the leader, the chairperson understands how to direct the meeting in a way that achieves maximum participation by the attendees while completing agenda items and accomplishing objectives.

If you lead a meeting, tie your opening statements directly to the purpose of the meeting itself. Your energy and attitude will set the tone and provide momentum for others. An enthusiastic opening line that set the stage for everyone to participate might be:

"Welcome everyone, I am happy that you could all make it today and I look forward to everyone providing input to the discussion. Our objective is to make a decision about the resources we will need to complete this project."

You can see how this opening line linguistically energizes the meeting and sends the message that everyone is expected to participate.

Many meetings are held to discuss sensitive issues, such as a staff disciplinary meeting. It may be useful to have a neutral facilitator to help mediate. Generally, the facilitator-leader sets the agenda, coaches participants, and guides the pacing. As a facilitator, the chairperson encourages participants to focus on the issues at hand, assigns priorities and guides everyone to contribute in a positive way. Here are a few facilitator guidelines:

- Invite comments and ideas from the group

- Record and display the group comments regarding action plans and solutions
- Invite participants to prioritize the action plan to include:
    o Action steps
    o Materials & Information
    o Schedules
    o Costs / Resources
- Describe Tasks & Who's responsible
- Gain commitment

As the meeting progresses, the facilitator-leader will insure understanding by clarifying key points throughout, and move the attendees from topic to topic based upon the timelines. Finally, the leader will move the meeting to a close by summarizing and reviewing commitments, decisions and action items.

A Briefing on Group Dynamics

Many managers ask me what to do about someone who dominates the meeting and won't give others a chance to speak. We've all met those kinds of people, the ones who may enter the room late, hog a conversation, or blast out their views at every turn whether their opinion is solicited or not. Although perceived as difficult, such individuals can be managed. In this situation, a leader can interject when there is a pause and say, *"Thank you very much for your contribution so far, and now let's see if anyone else would like to comment."*

Furthermore, I have found that internal processors tend to participate less in meetings because they need time to think things through before they will venture to comment. This is another reason why it is vital to distribute the agenda and materials *in advance* of the meeting. The Internal processor can review the documents before the meeting and gather their thoughts, thereby enabling their active participation.

I use a **round robin process** to open up the dialogue. I may start by saying, *"This next topic affects each department, so it is important that everyone provides input. We will go around the room and each person will get a chance to speak. If you are not ready to say anything, then say you are not ready and we will go to the next person."*

There are times when the chairperson is also a participant. In this case, the chairperson needs to switch hats so that the group knows he/she is providing an opinion or sharing their expertise. All the rules of the meeting apply to the chair the same as they do with other participants. Model all the meeting behaviours you are responsible for upholding.

As the chair, you also must be careful to not dominate the conversation, go off on tangents or have side bar conversations. If you do, others will follow you and the work at hand will not get done.

Step 12: Review effectiveness at the end of meetings.

If you plan to implement some or all of these steps to improve your workplace meetings, you need to build time into the agenda so everyone can have a moment to reflect. I usually add an agenda item at the end called *Meeting Effectiveness Review*. The meeting's effectiveness can be reviewed and suggestions made to improve the next meeting.

> *Here are some of the questions you might want to use for the review:*
>
> Did we have too many topics?
>
> Did we take too long for topics?
>
> Did we keep on track and not go off on tangents?
>
> Are there topics that should have been discussed outside the meeting?
>
> Did participants come prepared and bring their reports?
>
> Did everyone contribute to the meeting discussion?
>
> Were there **sidebar conversations** (i.e. people talking to each other)?
>
> Did we manage distractions such as cell phones, entering and leaving, etc.?
>
> Did we start and end on time?

Making Powerful Presentations

Presentations made with passion will be more engaging than presentations made with poise.

Passion is contagious, so choose subjects where you have a genuine interest or where you have specialized knowledge. Your passion for the topic will show when you present, and this will ignite your audience. Telling a story about your subject is the most powerful way to get people to relate to you. Make a plot that include humour, suspense, conflict and resolution. Always make your presentation relevant to your audience through the incorporation of examples pertinent to them, or relate back to their knowledge.

You are encouraged to set clear *expectations* and *objectives* for your presentation so that the audience will know exactly where you are taking them. Then, follow the four proven steps for preparing and delivering your presentation. According to Dale Carnegie, you should to *plan* your topics, *prepare* the materials, *practice* your delivery, and finally *present* the topics.

Concept building is the framework for describing each topic effectively. Concept building requires that you deliver your message in three main steps as defined below:

1. **Set up** your topic by telling the audience *why* they should learn about the topic. You need an *attention-getter* such as a quote, story or unusual statistic. Even showing an image could work, then describing it with an *engaging statement* telling how it relates to the topic.

In your setup you can use analogies and metaphors, show how you will solve a problem, provide an audience-relevant example, or show the final product you are building up to during the presentation.

2. **Deliver** your topic by *defining* the new concepts in plain language that your audience understands. In this step you will *show* how the subject relates to the audience. You can also create an *experiential* exercise to enable direct participant discovery of key aspects of the topic.

3. **Recap** your topic by *summarizing* or *restating* the key points, asking your audience to provide their own examples of their experience with the topic, or do a verbal test by prompting the attendees with a question.

Avoid the following common pitfalls: unclear purpose, illogical flow of ideas, giving too many details, not preparing, thereby appearing nervous, lack of data to backup your points, not making it relevant to the audience, and lack of enthusiasm and passion.

Follow these guidelines to create greater impact in all your presentations.

CHAPTER SIXTEEN

Leadership, Influence and Change

Leadership has been described as the process of social influence where one person can enlist the assistance and support of others in the accomplishment of a common goal. Leaders carry out this task by applying their leadership attributes, such as shared values and beliefs, trust and communication skills.

Think about someone in your life who you feel is a great leader. Would you agree that they are also a great communicator? The best leaders in the world are master communicators. They are able to articulate their vision to their teams through expressive language that inspires and motivates. These leaders understand how to accommodate for all the different styles of communication. They are proficient at navigating difficult situations when conflict arises to threaten team cohesiveness.

I believe that there are six principles that contribute to leadership competency and that you need to develop to enhance your leadership capacity. The six principles are:

1. Engage people first
2. Communicate frequently
3. Adapt to the situation
4. Manage thyself
5. Demonstrate resilience
6. Navigate change

Principle 1: Engage People First

Four years ago I was asked to conduct a competency review on a manager to determine where he might need some training and development. I set up an online review to measure his core competencies. To my surprise, he scored high on the most important competencies needed to perform well in the job. He was highly detail-oriented and had great analytical skills. So why was he not delivering at the standard required by his company?

After I interviewed him, the reason became apparent. I discovered that he had a high need for **affiliation**. This meant that he wanted to have regular and periodic contact with people throughout the day. However, the job required that he spend most of the day reviewing project reports to analyze progress and then alert his team via email if any issues came up. He was managing a virtual team – all the members were scattered across the globe in the U.S., Canada, India and parts of South America. He spent most of his work time in isolation and not interacting with fellow workers, which meant his affiliation need was not being fulfilled. As a result of months of being disconnected from others, he began to lose focus and took more and more breaks to talk with family and friends. He also began to wander around the small office, dropping in to chat with the other managers.

My final diagnosis was that the job lacked the right motivational factors to engage and reward him on a personal level, and so we implemented **virtual meetings** – these are meetings in which the parties are in different locations and use Internet-based technology, video-conferencing or teleconference to connect – where he met with his team on a weekly basis. He also began periodic one-on-one video conferences with key staff. His performance improved substantially once these changes were made and he had regular connections with his team. This example teaches us about the importance of motivation. Even with the right qualification, experience and skills, I have seen individuals underperform when their motivational needs are not met by the job.

Engaging the people in your organization is the first and most essential thing a leader can do. Even though an astute leader may be adept at recognizing when a team member lacks motivation, it is important to have a simple model to codify one's observations of the person to determine how they could be motivated. One such model is called the McClelland Theory of Needs, otherwise known as the acquired-needs theory.

In this theory, psychologist David McClelland describes three primary categories of needs that motivate people: **the need for achievement, for power and for affiliation**. McClelland feels that people grow into these needs depending upon their life experiences. Their motivation and effectiveness on the job is based upon how the job allows the individual to experience fulfillment of these needs.

Motivation factors are a need to feel a certain way. Those motivated by achievement need to feel a sense of accomplishment and success. Those motivated by power need to feel a sense of control and being in charge of things. Finally, those motivated by affiliation need to feel a sense of connection with those around them.

The need for **achievement** is that internal drive to excel and have personal accomplishments that are measured against a set of standards. Someone who has a high need for achievement will constantly be looking for the next challenge in order to prove to themselves that they can have success no matter the obstacle.

These individuals want to work at tasks that are not too easy or too hard. The challenge gives them the opportunity to stretch themselves and develop new skills. These are the people you see with day-timers filled with to-dos, or who are constantly making checklists. One of the best things for an achievement-motivated individual is the feeling they get when they check off items on the list at the end of the day. High achievers need to be given regular feedback so they can see the progress of their work.

A great leader will show appreciation to those who have a high achievement need by recognizing their work and giving them credit for their accomplishments. One thing to watch for with high achievers is that they typically want to work on their own. High achievement managers may work in silos because they are so caught up in making their own team success. A **silo** is a word used to depict the lack of cooperation, communication or common goals between departments in an organization, which results in a fragmented organization.

A couple of years ago I worked with a director of a community agency who could not get her managers to work well as a cohesive team. Each manager was a high performer in their own department, but inter-departmental accomplishments were lagging behind. The Director needed these managers to come together as a high performing group for the good of the organization.

I spent time with each manager, helping them to complete a motivational factors survey. We discovered that all the managers had a high score in their need for achievement. The Director was the only one with a high score for affiliation. She realized that it was up to her to get all her departmental managers working toward the organizational objectives rather than working as isolated islands.

I facilitated a workshop where all managers worked together to developed a plan for horizontal integration of team activities. They created both formal and informal activities such as cross-functional meetings to reduce the silo effect.

Those with a high need for **affiliation** require an environment where individuals are friendly. They desire a workplace that is harmonious and where there are positive interpersonal relationships among team members. Individuals with this motivational factor will go out of their way to do favours for others in order to gain their trust and acceptance. They are great team players who are happy to comply with organizational norms. You can count on these individuals to readily share the cultural norms that help in the socialization of new staff.

To keep those who have a need for affiliation motivated, we must create work situations where they have opportunities for a high level of personal interaction. Jobs such as customer service or call centres, where there is a greater volume of people interactions, are ideal jobs for individuals with a strong need for affiliation. A sense of isolation and loneliness are prevalent among individuals who have a high affiliation need and are put in positions where they have to work alone. As discussed in an earlier example, it can lead to dysfunctional work habits.

Let's turn our attention to the individuals in our organizations who have a high **power** need. We know that there are people who, on a personal level, have a desire to influence the behaviour of others. This can be a very positive attribute if it translates into what we call *institutional power* rather than a need to have personal power over others. A desire for institutional power means that individuals aspire to organize and influence others toward the completion of organizational objectives. Leaders with high institutional power needs tend to be better at coordinating teams than those who have a personal need for power.

If a person is not having their need for power met, he/she may manifest derailing behaviours in their teams by bossing around peers and challenging the formal leader. I consulted with a supervisor who had a woman in her group who would frequently hijack the weekly team meeting.

To tackle this destructive behaviour, I instructed the supervisor to put her in charge of something innocuous such as being the time keeper. The woman quickly agreed to do it. At first she was very strict with the times, cutting people off in the middle of their sentence to tell them that their time was up, but gradually, and with some coaching, she became a very effective time keeper. She also eventually took charge of making the minutes. Meetings were substantially improved with her efforts.

You should work toward harnessing this type of individual's desire to have greater responsibility by putting them in charge of a small project. Wherever possible, allow them to direct their own activities, making sure that you first define what is required – but giving them the space to figure out how to make it happen. Also, try to provide these individuals with more options and choices on the job.

Considerations for Management

Management must recognize that people are motivated uniquely, and as such they need to develop environments and practices that are varied to meet their motivational differences. In summary, the three motivational needs are:

Need for achievement – The drive to excel and achieve beyond a set of defined standards, and to have success

Need for power – The need to influence others to move toward a goal and to be in charge of specific objectives

Need for affiliation – The desire for friendly and close interpersonal interactions

To engage individuals with these motivational factors, managers should follow these guidelines. Specifically, employees:

- *With a high achievement need* should be put in positions where they will have challenging but achievable tasks. They will need regular verbal and written feedback, recognition and credit for their accomplishments. These individuals don't mind working on their own.
- *With a high affiliation need* should be put in positions where there is opportunity for team work and cooperative situations. These individuals don't mind frequent interactions with the public.
- *With a high power (specifically institutional power) need* should be provided opportunities to lead and manage others. These individuals will be comfortable taking on the responsibility to influence others toward a goal.

Extrinsic vs. Intrinsic Motivations

The motivation needs we have discussed are intrinsic motivators, which are a person's internal desire to perform a task due to their interest, challenge and personal satisfaction. It's been proven that after a certain level of income – which varies by profession – extrinsic motivators (like money), no longer serve as primary motivators of work behaviour. Extrinsic motivation comes from outside the person and includes such tangible rewards such as pay, bonuses and other perks. Hence, leaders much rely on intrinsic motivation to produce sustainable efforts from their personnel.

Here's a list of additional ways to increase intrinsic motivation in employees:

- Give them a sense of choice; this is especially important for those with a high need for power
- Empower people and delegate tasks; this will engage those who need achievement and power
- Give them a sense of competence; this will engage those who need a sense of achievement
- Support and coach people; this will engage those who have a need for affiliation
- Give them a sense of meaningfulness; this motivates all equally
- Sense of progress; it engages those with an achievement and affiliation need
- Monitor, give feedback and reward people – works well for all
- Inspire people by modelling desired behaviours – works well for everyone

Principle 2: Communicate Frequently

The biggest complaint I hear from staff at the many team building programs I have conducted is that they wished that senior leadership teams would communicate with them more frequently. Great leaders have an open communication policy. They believe that all information that affects the organization must be shared in a sincere and transparent manner so that everyone will have what they need to perform at optimum levels.

The way to keep abreast of what is going on in your corporation is to communicate with your staff; speak with your customers and with everyone who could have an impact on your company. Create a means for two-way dialogue, such as email and social networking technology.

Listen to those on the frontline to gain a handle on key issues that can propel your company forward. Make time to talk to all your teams regularly. Find ways to inform and invite communication on daily, weekly and monthly basis.

Conveying complex information takes a special knack for using what someone already knows to help them understand what you want them to know. An effective communicator will use examples, analogies and metaphors to make information more understandable. Asking the listener to restate your message ensures they got it.

There are various forms of communication that managers use to get their point across to others. Managers use **mass communication** such as public presentations, posters, ads, newsletters and annual reports to communicate information in a global way to a larger population of stakeholders – **corporate stakeholders** are people, groups, board of directors, and customers who are affected or who can affect the organization.

Next we have **interpersonal communication**, which is the transmission of information to fewer people. Interpersonal communication differs from other forms of communication in that there are fewer participants involved than in mass communication, the interactions are in close physical proximity to each other, there are many sensory channels used, and feedback is immediate. Interpersonal communication is what occurs between managers and subordinates, peer-groups and can be up and down or laterally across the organizational chart.

One form of interpersonal communication that is worth mentioning is the **grapevine**. This is a random and informal type of communication that is prone to having inaccuracies. Another term that is use interchangeable with grapevine is **gossip**. Gossip is idle rumors about organizational issues or personal details about others in the company. Gossip typically involves the sharing of information that has not yet been confirmed to be true and as such could be damaging to the individuals and the company.

Reaching out to your people will require the utilization of all these forms of communication –mass and interpersonal – at the appropriate times. Yes, even gossip could be useful with informal influencers spreading it along the grapevine. In this case the leader could plant a **meme** – an idea, belief, behaviour or style that spreads rapidly from person to person within a culture.

Principle 3: Adapt to the Situation

Leadership style is the manner and approach that leaders take in providing direction, implementing plans, and motivating people. Kurt Lewin (1939) led a study to identify different styles of leadership.

This early study has been very influential in establishing three major leadership styles identified in the subjects. The three major styles of leadership are:

- Authoritarian / autocratic
- Participative / democratic
- Delegative / Free Reign

Authoritarian / Autocratic Style

Authoritarian or autocratic leaders are directive in their approach. Leaders *tell* their team members and employees what they want done and how they want it accomplished, without getting the advice of their followers. This directive style is characterized by leaders who make decisions for others - and expect followers or subordinates to follow their instructions.

An authoritative style is appropriate for certain business conditions. Specifically, this directive method works best when you have all the information to solve the problem, you are short on time, it is a crisis situation, or your team members / employees are highly motivated.

Individuals who are not good leaders may appear to be using an autocratic approach because they boss people around through raising their voice, using demeaning language, and leading by threats and exerting their power. This represents a misuse of the authoritarian style and has no place in a leader's repertoire.

Autocratic leaders can be heard saying, "I want you to assign Mary to deal with this staffing problem."

Participative (Democratic)

Participative leaders will tend to involve others at various stages of the decision-making process, including consulting staff for key facts and determining who should be involved. However, the leader maintains the final decision-making authority once they feel they have received all the information they need. Sometimes those with an autocratic leadership style might judge participative leaders as being weak-willed, but it is a proven fact that people will support and take greater ownership of decisions that they are involved in. Therefore, a democratic leader is using the strength of all his/her team and will be respected for it.

This leadership approach is perfect for situations where you have only a part of the information required to make a decision. In this case, your employees have important data or opinions that will help you make a better quality decision. Participative leaders will tend to surround themselves with employees who are knowledgeable subject matter experts and able to contribute skillfully to solving organizational problems. Using this style is of mutual benefit — it allows employees to become stronger team members and allows you to make better decisions.

Democratic leaders can be heard saying, "Let's work together to solve this staffing problem."

Delegative (Free Reign)

In the Delegative style, the leader allows their employees to make most of the decisions; in other words, they have free reign. However, the leader will still take responsibility for all decisions made. This is an effective approach when team members are able to analyze the situation and determine what needs to be done and how to do it. Like participative leaders, delegative leaders will also tend to hire people who are experts and who have specialized knowledge that they might not possess. You cannot do everything, so it is essential to develop techniques to manage the delegative process, such as setting priorities and following up on delegated tasks.

This approach works well when you have established trust and have confidence in your subordinates. Delegative leaders can be heard saying, "You can take care of the staffing problem while I go to the board meeting."

Think of these leadership styles on a continuum, with Authoritative at one end and Delegative at the opposite. Your dominant leadership style lands somewhere on this continuum. Recognizing your leadership style is essential to developing a conscious awareness of your specific approach to people on the job or in your personal life. Learning to be flexible in your leadership approach is vital in today's diverse workforce.

Some examples where each approach might be appropriate include:
- Using an authoritarian style on a new employee who is learning the job. The leader is competent and a good coach. The employee is motivated to learn a new skill.
- Using a participative style with a team of workers who know their job. The leader knows the problem, but does not have all the information. The team members / employees know their jobs and want to become part of the team.
- Using a delegative style with a worker who knows more about the job than you. You cannot do everything and the employee needs to take

ownership of her job. In addition, this allows you to be at other places, doing other things.
- Using all three: Telling your team members / employees that a procedure is not working correctly and a new one must be established (authoritarian). Asking for their ideas and input on creating a new procedure (participative). Delegating tasks in order to implement the new procedure (delegative).

What Leadership Style Are You?

As you read descriptions of the different styles, can you determine your dominant approach? Are you more directive, more participative, or do you prefer to fully delegate to others?

My Leadership style is (write your guess in the space below):

Modern Leadership Styles

A good leader uses all three styles, depending on situational factors such as the knowledge of the followers, the leader's needs, and the circumstances. Ineffective leaders tend to stick to their preferred style across all situations, dealing with everyone the same way.

In the mid 1970s a new model called the Situational Leadership Model was developed by a professor called Paul Hersey. Later on he updated the model and Ken Blanchard also outlined a similar model.

The main gist of the **situational leadership model** is that no single style is best for leadership. Successful leaders should adapt to the environment to ensure their approach is task-relevant. Our modern economy is dependent on highly educated knowledge workers who are self-managing and willing to take full accountability for the job.

Leaders need to be ready to vary their leadership approach with a new type of workforce who dislikes micro-management. No one style of leadership pertains to all given workplace situations, so the effective leader must flex to the people, task and function that needs to be accomplished.

Situational Leadership relies on effectiveness in four communication components:
- communicating expectations
- listening
- delegating
- providing feedback

Facilitated leadership is an approach I have advocated for managers to adopt for many years. In our new economy, facilitated leadership is a perfect approach that combines coaching, guiding and influencing to move others toward gaining their own understanding and ownership of tasks. Leaders guide others toward self-discovery through the use of questions that direct a person's mind to explore and discover the answers on their own. Often these answers are obvious to the facilitated leader, but he/she knows that people are more likely to believe their own thoughts than what they are told. Facilitated leaders make great coaches.

Principle 4: Manage Thyself

Self-management or self-leadership is one of the most important competencies that every employer looks for. This is especially true for managers and leaders. Self-leadership means that you are adept at:

- Setting your own goals, planning and implementing tasks on a timeline
- Evaluating your own performance
- Solving your own problems
- Motivating yourself
- Taking initiative
- Self-reinforcing
- Providing your own sense of reward and feedback on how tasks are carried out

How would you rate yourself from 1 to 5 on these above dimensions of self-leadership, (where one is low and 5 is high)? Would you score a 4 or higher on most criteria? Your leadership potential is directly correlated with high scores in self-management.

Leaders can help employees to develop their self-management skills through modeling behaviours such as self-observation, setting challenging personal goals, and being self-directed. As a leader in your organization, you are encouraged to use the following to help team members increase their ability in this area:

- Encourage employees to set their own goals
- Encourage the use of self-rewards to strengthen and increase self-managing behaviours
- Create positive thought patterns by utilizing mental imagery and self-talk to further stimulate self-motivation

Principle 5: Demonstrate Resilience

Several years ago the career centre of a local university was undergoing a major change in the organizational culture mandated by a newly appointed director. Employee reactions ranged from anxiety to excitement, causing a lot of ambiguity in the department. The group's manager decided that the team needed to develop their resilience. Resilience is defined as:
- An occurrence of rebounding or springing back
- Recovering readily from adversity
- Ability to weather tribulation without cracking

I facilitated a workshop in resilience and navigating change to help team members enhance their capacity to move forward, and found that people want to follow those who have confidence and strength. Resilient leaders help to reduce anxiety in the organization through their expression of courage and versatility. Great leaders must demonstrate resilience in the face of change to instill hope in employees.

Management teams should facilitate conversations between teams to expose differences and allow for a shared understanding of how things can be adjusted for new realities. People at all levels in the organization can develop their capacity to reframe situations, move beyond obstacles, be persistent and take initiative. These are the ingredients of highly-resilient individuals.

Principle 6: Navigate Change

An aging workforce, retiring senior management and succession planning, new-fangled technological demands, economic downturns, downsizing companies, globalization and outsourcing are among the many challenges facing modern organizations.

Organizational Change Management is a structured approach to transitioning and transforming individuals, teams and organizations from a current state to a desired future state. This is characterized by a shift in people's behaviours and attitudes toward adopting innovative practices. I believe that this requires a *compelling vision* that pulls employees forward to a position where they can feel included, and part of realizing the organizational mission. Effective leaders must communicate organi-zational objectives so the employees will know what direction the company is moving toward.

Change occurs when there is an imbalance between the current state and a shift in the new environment. Change can really impact individuals within the organization, and effective change management requires an understanding of the possible effects of change upon people, as well as managing potential sources of resistance to that shift. "People who are confronted by change will experience a form of culture-shock as established patterns of corporate life are altered, or viewed by people as being threatened. Employees will typically experience a form of grief or loss (Stuart, 1995)."

In my experience, I have seen that when an organization shifts, the staff often experience a crisis of identity or a sense of lost competency. Therefore, leaders should see that an integral component of managing change is to focus on the people side of the business.

Management's responsibility is to detect trends in the macro-environment as well as in the micro-environment to be able to identify emerging issues and initiate programs that *motivate* people to participate in making change happen. People will proactively engage in the organization when they are inspired by their management team.

A change management initiative should include an *environmental scan* which can reveal these triggers and other important indicators and best practices that could be adopted to enhance the effectiveness of the change process. It is also important to estimate what impact a change will likely have on an employee's behaviour patterns, work processes, technological requirements, and motivation.

Management must assess employee reactions, and craft a change program that will provide support as personnel go through the process of accepting what has to happen. The program must then be promoted, disseminated throughout the organization, implemented, monitored for effectiveness, and tracked and adjusted when necessary.

Almost every business owner I have worked with recently has expressed concern about the speed of the change they are experiencing. They feel change is more rapid than ever in history. Organizations feel as if they are treading water while trying to keep up with these turbulent times. The implications for businesses are dramatic, and call for leaders who have versatile capabilities to keep their companies succeeding.

ADAPT™ FRAMEWORK

In response to the many requests to assist companies with their change management initiative, I developed a framework called ADAPT™ to guide the change process. The building blocks of the ADAPT™ Framework are:
- **Awareness** of what and why change is happening
- **Decision** to adapt and not resist the change
- **Ability** to participate fully due to development of new competencies and behavioural shifts
- **Progress** is measured and sustainability promoted
- **Tracking** to manage the process of evolution

An expanded discussion of this framework is beyond the scope of this book, but I have included it to illustrate the importance of having a methodology to manage change. A more detailed breakdown and analysis of this structure can be found in my upcoming book on leadership.

It is important not to lose faith in yourself and your team's ability to weather challenges. According to a 1991 study, some of the skills that accompany success are:

1. Curiosity: exploring new learning opportunities
2. Persistence: exerting effort despite setbacks
3. Flexibility: changing attitudes and circumstances
4. Optimism: viewing new opportunities as possible and attainable
5. Risk Taking: taking action in the face of uncertain outcomes

Hope is something we must all have to strive toward our future goals. People who maintain a high degree of hope are more likely to be successful at many different levels, such as health, general happiness and achievement.

It has been said that hope contains two sets of beliefs: first, the assurance that there will be ways around whatever obstacle or difficulty we encounter, and second, the belief in one's own ability to solve problems and achieve results.

At the individual level, hope happens when people:
- Are aware of and develop confidence in their own abilities and skills
- See purpose and meaning in their efforts
- Feel they have responsibility for decision-making
- Believe that they can make a difference
- Are supported and encouraged in their efforts

At the societal level, hope builds when people see:
- Leaders who care for the welfare of others
- Consistency and follow-through from leaders; promises that are kept

In Closing

Organizations exist within a dynamic environment that is subject to shifts due to the impact of various change triggers, such as evolving technologies, social shifts, and other trends. To continue to operate effectively within these chaotic times, organizations must be able to change and adapt themselves in response to internal and external pressures based upon new regulations, economic trends and competitive forces.

Employees need time for information sharing and to ask questions about how doing things the "new way" will affect them. They need to share their concerns about what they may be losing. Leaders must help staff understand that there is a natural mourning period that cannot be skipped when change happens. Acknowledgement of the emotional and mental shifts that are taking place with people in organizations today must occur.

If people are reluctant to change, the organization's capacity to evolve is greatly hindered. Even in cases where formal authority is utilized and sanctions are imposed to get people to comply with what they are told to do, we find that good people leave – making it harder for the organization to adjust. This is a major threat for organizations where the subject matter expertise of highly experienced personnel is almost impossible to replace.

We know that these individuals typically do not respond well to being "told" to change – they need to know what the proposed changes are, why they are taking place, and how they will enhance the individuals' personal, professional and social goals. Research shows that we are happiest when we feel part of a larger community.

Great leaders need to become *chameleons* – shifting and adapting their communication, motivational and leadership approach to connect everyone in the organization and get them inspired to come along for the journey. What is *your* organization doing to celebrate and reward those who readily embrace the challenges of change?

Behavioural flexibility is the most powerful response to this ever-changing and diverse world. This requires mindsight. *Mindsight* is your mind's ability to see itself, which is the object of study in an emerging field called Interpersonal Neurobiology. This field is evolving as part of the science of personal transformation. Mindsight provides a lens through which we can understand our inner workings in order to transform ourselves and enhance our relationships.

The Communication Chameleon was written to enhance your mindsight so you can understand yourself better, thereby evolving your skills and mindset to communicate with others more meaningfully. I trust that you will continue to apply all that you have learned well beyond the turning of this last page.

APPENDIX I

Executive Summaries

CHAPTER 1: The Mind Does the Listening

Our mind is the filter through which all stimuli are passed and interpreted. The beliefs, thoughts, and things we say are formulated to a large extent in our subconscious, which might cause us to delete, distort and generalize reality. In other words, it is the mind that does the listening.

Often the way we interpret and react to the people around us seems to spring automatically from a deep inner place, without our conscious control. These responses are habitual due to automaticity. We often repeat and replay conversations in a ritualistic manner, causing reduced effectiveness. The questions we ask ourselves cause our mind to seek answers that may or may not support our well-being. We must find a way to interrupt the pattern of such repetitive behaviors in order to be a better communicator.

CHAPTER 2: Reality is Relative

Perception is the process in which we interpret and organize stimuli to understand and give meaning to the experiences we are having. In other words, perception is the process by which sensory stimulation is translated into experience. Our perception of the world is primarily based upon how we process the sensory input from our eyes, ears, nose, tongue and touch. It is well known that what we perceive is often different from what might really be going on. There are multiple factors that affect our perceptual filters, including the situation / setting, the other person, and the perceiver's own mind.

Your perception of *reality* is *relative* to who you are and how you view the world. We create our own reality by choosing what we focus on. As a result, many misunderstandings may rise between people due to **perceptual errors**, a common barrier to effective communication.

We are fortunate to have a part of the brain that takes on the role of gate-keeping to help us focus our attention, the **Reticular Activating System.** The RAS helps us focus by screening the type of information that is allowed to get through to the conscious mind, while filtering out other stimuli.

CHAPTER 3: Emotions get in the way (Emotional Hijack)

Today's modern workplace has many psychological dangers which can cause us to experience a great deal of emotional crisis. We have more to do in less time, colleagues are in competition with us for scarce resources, the economic situation has us fearing for our jobs.

We experience fight-or-flight symptoms, along with accompanying emotional responses, when we are stressed. We might feel a rapid heartbeat, freeze up and breathe shallowly as stress hormones are released – all being reactions we would naturally experience if we were under physical danger. This creates a state of emotional hijack in which we are ruled by our physiological response. Over the years I've learned that it is impossible to have a rational conversation if you have not acknowledged and validated the intense emotions that are present.

People want to know that you understand how they feel before they are able to move on. The second step in overcoming an emotional situation is to listen and acknowledge the other person's feelings and to express and validate your own.

CHAPTER 4: Formative Experiences and Anchors

Communication mastery begins with the conversation you have with yourself.

Our formative experiences contribute to the main components of our core belief system. These beliefs become the foundation of our how we interpret external stimuli and perceive our reality. Many of our subconscious habits and aspects of our self-image are laid down during our formative years – not only our developmentally-formative years (birth to age ten), but also the first encounters that will come to form the foundation of our belief system – the friends we have in school, the social and community groups we belong to, our first love and our first job.

Stimuli-response pairings are triggered by **anchors**. Anchors can serve to trigger positive or negative behaviours. We know that our formative experiences contribute to our programmed subconscious behaviours. It is vital to gain a clear understanding of how your past has embedded subconscious anchors that trigger specific reactions in you. Then look at how they are related to your interactions with others.

CHAPTER 5: Self-identity

Our self-identity is our internal multi-faceted model and understanding of the 'self' as it relates to a number of characteristics such as gender, intellect, race, skills, abilities, competencies, physical characteristics and the personality we've identify for ourselves.

Arguments can often leave us feeling disturbed about how we appear to others. Will they think we are unstable, or mean-spirited or unreasonable? Unraveling our inner workings and gaining knowledge of where we have vulnerabilities in our self-identity is the best way to arm ourselves against behaving in ways that cause us to become off balanced. If we have foreknowledge of the extreme tendencies we have inherited from our experiences, we can avoid acting in inappropriate ways.

CHAPTER 6: Behavioural Flexibility using DISC Communication Styles

Behavioural flexibility is the single most important aptitude you will need to develop in order to achieve communications mastery. In today's diverse society, you must become a chameleon in how you communicate.

The specific framework for developing behavioural flexibility is the DISC Communications model that corresponds to four primary factors:
1. Dominance (referred to as Red) – relates to control and strong assertiveness
2. Influence (referred to as Yellow) - relates to social connections and conversations
3. Steadiness (referred to as Green) – relates to patience and predictability
4. Compliance (referred to as Blue) - relates to structure, procedures and analyzing

We predict the behaviour and flex to the person we are talking to by scanning for these attributes:

Blue (Task-oriented, details) Introverted & Task-oriented Internal processing	Red (Task oriented, no details) Extroverted & Task-oriented External processing
Green (People-oriented, details) Introverted & People-oriented Internally processing	Yellow (People-oriented, no details) Extroverted & People-oriented External processing

CHAPTER 7: Team Building with the Colours

Clashes occur between different communications styles due to differences stemming from a perceived incompatibility in how team members complete tasks and behave in interpersonal situations. Use the knowledge of the communication do's and don'ts to converse most effectively with each style.

CHAPTER 8: Learning styles (Representational Systems)

In NLP, the learning model is described as our **representational systems**, also known as *sensory modalities*. The representational system defines how our minds process information through the use of our senses. The model's acronym is **VAKOG**, which refers to **visual, auditory, kinesthetic, olfactory and gustatory**.

Visual learners want information presented to them so that they can see it; **Aural learners** (also called **Auditory**) want to hear and listen; **Kinesthetic learners** (also called Tactile) want to experience the learning.

Most recently in NLP a new emerging learning style has been defined as Auditory Digital. These individuals have a preference for dialogue that is presented in a logical and sequential manner.

CHAPTER 9: Building Subconscious Rapport

Establishing and maintaining rapport with someone is the foundation of effective communication. Rapport establishes trust which builds relationships. *When people are like each other, they tend to like each other.*

Our subconscious mind provides constant surveillance of our environment, looking for what is *different*. Different means unpredictable, and therefore our subconscious will interpret different as unsafe. If we see something familiar, our subconscious will relax. This is part of the underlying psychology that makes rapport-building work. If I can make you feel at ease and that we are alike, you will trust me. With this trust we can have great communication and develop a deeper connection.

Rapport is the feeling of being in *sync* with each other. *Mirroring and matching* the behaviour of the person with whom you are interacting is the most instant way to create rapport. To **mirror** someone's behaviour, do exactly what they are doing. If they cross their arms, you should be crossing your arms; if they cross their legs, do it also. To **match** someone's behaviour means that you are approximating their gestures.

CHAPTER 10: The Importance of Non-Verbal Communication

Dr. Albert Mehrabian was able to demonstrate the importance of non-verbal communication in a study where he developed what is now called the 7%-38%-55% rule. The 7% refers to words, 38% refers to the tonality and 55% refers to body language. Mehrabian studied the importance of verbal and non-verbal communication, and found that effective and meaningful communication about our feelings requires that these three components are congruent. In situations where there is ambigiuity between our words, the body language and our tone (i.e. when our verbal and non-verbal elements do not match), people will most likely trust the non-verbal information.

Developing a solid foundation for reading body language is an indispensable component in all aspects of communication. Whether you are about to do an interview, have a meeting and or participate in negotiations, understanding body language can give you the winning edge.

CHAPTER 11: Conversational Self-Defense

Defensiveness is characterized by us being off-balanced, flustered and under emotional hijack. As in physical self-defense, **conversational self-defense** is the antidote for difficult

conversations and it can be broken down into the following required elements.
You need to:
- Remain emotionally-controlled and grounded
- Stay self-aware of your contribution
- Have mental clarity

CHAPTER 12: Reframing: A Tool For Change

If you narrow your frame-of-reference with limiting beliefs, you will reduce what you see in a situation. When we reframe, we give ourselves the chance to see a situation from a different perspective. Reframing helps us to perceive, interpret, conclude and react to an experience in a different manner. **Reframing** expands your potential by giving you another way to think, feel, do, and ultimately choose how you respond to an experience.

CHAPTER 13: Powerful Negotiations in Seven Steps

Negotiation *is the process of communicating back and forth to reach a joint decision.*
A powerful negotiator will always have a game plan and a strategic approach to making the negotiations successful. In this chapter you will learn the seven steps toward powerful negotiations, which are:
1. Identify your objective
2. Prepare and research
3. Brainstorm alternative solutions
4. Plan your approach
5. Set the right atmosphere
6. Make it a problem-solving discussion
7. Move to a close

CHAPTER 14: Essential Interview Skills and Techniques

To be an excellent candidate, there are a variety of things you need to do to position yourself as a top choice. These include

activities *before the interview, during the interview* **and** *after the interview*. The most central aspect to being a strong interviewee is to be prepared. Preparation is the primary way to reduce anxiety. In career coaching, I instruct clients to:
- prepare the mind
- prepare the paper
- prepare the look
- prepare for questions

Behavioural style interviews have become very prevalent over the past 10 years. The theory behind behavioural interviewing is that the most accurate predictor of future performance is based upon how the person performed in the past. In this type of interview the interviewer describes a real on-the-job scenario and gauges if your answer demonstrates that you have the right experience in performing the relevant tasks.

CHAPTER 15: Masterful Meetings

I have developed the following twelve step guideline for planning and running meetings:

1. Only have a meeting if it is really necessary.
2. All meetings must have a clear objective or purpose.
3. Who should be involved in the meeting?
4. All meetings must have an agenda.
5. Assign and circulate relevant meeting information and reports prior to the meeting.
6. Meetings must start and end on time so as not to punish those who are punctual.
7. Meeting participants must be prepared to participate.
8. Meeting minutes (i.e. notes) must be recorded.
9. Meeting decisions must be documented.
10. Action items must be documented and followed up.
11. Have a strong chairperson or a neutral facilitator.
12. Review meeting effectiveness at the end.

In **Making Powerful Presentations** you are encouraged to set clear *expectations* and *objectives* for your presentation so that the audience will know exactly where you are taking them. Follow the four proven steps for preparing and delivering your presentation. According to Dale Carnegie, you should to *plan* your topics, *prepare* the materials, *practice* your delivery, and finally *present* the topics.

CHAPTER 16: Leadership, Influence and Change

There are six principles that contribute to leadership competency and that you need to develop to enhance your leadership capacity. These six principles are:
1. Engage people first
2. Communicate frequently
3. Adapt to the situation
4. Manage thyself
5. Demonstrate resilience
6. Navigate change

We discuss each of these six steps, defining and describing how to develop the skills to implement a new leadership approach. To engage individuals with these motivational factors, managers should follow these guidelines. Specifically those:

- *With a high achievement need* should be put in positions where they have challenging but achievable tasks. They will need regular verbal and written feedback, recognition and credit for their accomplishments. These individuals don't mind working on their own
- *With a high affiliation need* should be put in positions where there is opportunity for team work and cooperative situations. These individuals don't mind frequent interactions with the public.
- *With a high power (specifically institutional power) need* should be provided opportunities to lead and manage others. These individuals will be comfortable taking on the responsibility of influencing others toward a goal.

Leadership style is the manner and approach that leaders take in providing direction, implementing plans, and motivating people. Kurt Lewin (1939) led a study to identify different styles of leadership. This early study has been very influential in establishing three major leadership styles which were identified in the subjects.

The three major styles of leadership are:

- Authoritarian / autocratic
- Participative / democratic
- Delegative / Free Reign

APPENDIX II

Glossary

Active listening – also called **paraphrasing** - is a technique for listening and responding to another person that results in improved communication and understanding. To summarize, active listening involves:

1. Paraphrase the main point in your own words
2. Share your understanding of key ideas
3. Pause to allow the speaker to agree or disagree
4. Ask questions to clarify
5. Reflect back the speaker's feelings

Agendas are an instrument to keep meetings on track, both in terms of timing and topics.

Amygdala – Deep within our brain's temporal lobe there is an almond-shaped mass of nuclei called the amygdala. This part of the brain plays a primary role in the processing and storage of our emotional reactions. When we feel fear, the fear stimuli is processed by the amygdala, where they are associated with memories of the stimuli and a fear response is elicited.

Anchors are stimuli-response pairings that can be triggered intentionally or accidentally.

Auditory Digitals are individuals have a preference for dialogue that is presented in a logical and sequential manner.

Aural learners (also called **Auditory**) want to hear and listen in order to learn.

Authoritarian or autocratic leaders are directive in their approach and want to make their own decisions.

Automaticity is the ability to do things without occupying the mind because the behaviour has become a habit, an automatic response pattern. Automaticity is a form of deep subconscious learning (called subconscious competence) due to the repetition, reinforcement and practice of a specific behaviour or thought.

Attention bias is when you pay attention to certain details more so than others due to what you value or believe. This is potentially what is happening in an argument, where we are predisposed to pay attention to what we expect to hear.

Brainstorming is an effective way to generate lots of possible solutions and to evaluate the best among these ideas.

Behavioural flexibility is defined as the ability to shift our behaviour and communication style based upon the situation and the person with whom we are communicating. Behavioural flexibility is possible if we first understand ourselves and simultaneously have a process for reading others.

Behavioural style interviews have become very prevalent over the past 10 years. The theory behind behavioural interviewing is that the most accurate predictor of future performance is based upon how the person performed in the past, in a similar situation.

Cognitive bias is the tendency to process and filter information through our own experiences, likes and dislikes, is especially prevalent during arguments. We become more and more incapable to accurately process what the other person is trying to make us understand.

Cognitive Dissonance is the tension produced by holding two competing or conflicting thoughts in our minds at the same time.

Conditional offer is where you propose a set of conditions for each party in order for the deal to move forward. For instance you might say, "If you do X, then we will do Y." This gives you a way to gauge which conditions or options might be suitable to the other party.

Concessions are trade-offs where you give up or concede to part of your proposal in order to keep the negotiations moving

Corporate stakeholders are people, groups, board of directors, and customers who are affected or who can affect the organization

Defensiveness is characterized by us being off-balanced, flustered and under emotional hijack.

Delegative leaders allow their employees to make most of the decisions, in other words they have free reign.

Disassociation is a powerful technique for helping us to re-evaluate and **reframe** the events in our life by viewing them from different perspectives.

Emotional Hijack is a word used to describe the fear reaction which hijacks our higher thinking, leading us to interpret the situation in ways that dramatically skew our perception of reality. Our emotions grow out of control and we become hyper-sensitive to what is happening around us.

Emotional intelligence (EI) can be defined as the ability, skill, and a self-perceived ability to identify, assess, and control the emotions of oneself and others.

Emotional literacy is defined as the ability to understand your emotions, the ability to listen to others and empathize with their emotions, and the ability to express emotions productively.

Escalation of commitment is the tendency to put in more and more resources in an obvious losing proposition due to the time, effort, emotions and money that you have already invested.

External processors are people who like to think out loud.

Extroverts have a tendency to be gregarious and assertive, and are the first to introduce themselves in a room full of strangers. They are not shy or afraid to be in novel situations where they are required to be outgoing.

Empathetic listening is a way of listening and responding to the client that enhances mutual understanding.

Gambit is an opening action (strategy or tactic) or remark that is calculated to gain an advantage. A word that is commonly used in chess where the player has a planned series of moves at the beginning of the game such as an opening move in which a player makes a sacrifice (usually a pawn) for the sake of a compensating advantage. Simply put, a gambit is a trick to manipulate the outcome of the negotiations.

Gossip is idle rumors about organizational issues or personal details about others in the company.

Grapevine is a random and informal type of communication that is prone to having inaccuracies.

Hypothetical close is using a phrase such as "How would you feel if we settled on 20%?" then wait to see the person's response. A hypothetical close helps everyone to save face because it is not definite and can be taken off the table if you receive a negative response.

Interrupt the pattern is a way to change behaviour in order to break the cycle of the ritual.

Internal-processing means that the person will think things through before speaking up.

Ideomotor effect is a term that refers to the automatic muscular reflex response that occurs due to a thought. Under hypnosis I may prompt a client to indicate a "yes" or "no" response with a specific finger, or even to raise a hand if they feel any discomfort.

Introverts in contrast to extroverts, are individuals who appear to be more reserved and introspective. At a party full of strangers, an introvert prefers to stand back and observe the scene, waiting until someone else approaches them for an introduction.

Kinesthetic learners (also called tactile) want to experience the learning by doing an activity.

Leadership has been described as the process of social influence where one person can enlist the assistance and support of others in the accomplishment of a common goal.

Lobbying is the act of attempting to influence decisions or advocating for specific interests through pre-meetings and private conversations.

Meme is an idea, belief, behaviour or style that spreads from person to person within a culture.

Micro-behaviours to refer to the breaking down and describing of small changes in a person's actions such as shifting their posture, turning their head, yawning unexpectedly, sighing, and rolling their eyes.

Microexpressions are involuntary facial expressions which appear based upon the emotional state of the person.

Mirror neurons are a special class of brain cells that fire not only when an individual performs an action, but also when the individual observes someone else make the same movement.

Minutes describe the events of the meeting, including a list of attendees, a statement of the issues discussed by the participants, and related responses or decisions on these issues.

Need for achievement is the drive to excel and achieve beyond a set of standards and to have success.

Need for affiliation is the desire for friendly and close interpersonal interactions.

Need for power is the need to influence others to move toward a goal and to be in charge of specific objectives.

Negotiation is the process of communicating back and forth to reach a joint decision. Think of this as a special type of conversation in which both you and someone else mutually desire a positive outcome.

Neuro-Linguistic Programming (NLP) is a term was coined to describe the foundational belief of the model that there are connections between the neurological and linguistic processes, which form specific behavioural patterns that have been programmed in us based upon our life experiences.

Objective listening is our ability to listen to someone else's ideas or opinions, be open to accepting another's ideas to be as valid as ours, and possibly choosing their idea over our own.

Organizational Change Management is a structured approach to transitioning and transforming individuals, teams, and organizations from a current state to a desired future state.

Participative leaders will tend to involve others in various stages of the decision-making process.

Perception is the process in which we interpret and organize stimuli to understand and give meaning to the experiences we are having.

Psychological projection is when we deny our own feelings and subconscious characteristics but assign them to someone else. Projection reduces negative feelings by allowing the expression of the unwanted unconscious impulses without letting the conscious mind recognize them.

Phatic communication is another word for small talk which can be verbal or non-verbal. The term phatic (from the Greek *phanein*: to show oneself) describes expressions that are used as a courtesy rather than to convey meaning or information.

Rapport is the feeling of being in *sync* with each other.

Read/Write learners want to read, then rewrite in order to learn

Reframing expands your potential by giving you another way to think, feel, do and ultimately choose how you will respond to an experience. New perspectives will create new possibilities.

Representational system defines how our minds process information through the use of our senses.

Resume – A **chronological** style resume lists your work experience in reverse chronological format, with the most recent job listed first in the experience section and working backwards. A **functional** resume lists your work experience in specific skill clusters in order to focus attention on different areas of expertise.

Reticular Activating System, also known as the RAS. The reticular activating system helps mediate transitions from relaxed wakefulness to periods of high attention. The RAS is made up of billions of nerve cells that are densely packed at the central part of the brainstem. The RAS helps us focus by screening the type of information that is allowed to get through to the conscious mind, while filtering out other stimuli.

Scope creep is a circumstance where you go beyond initially agreed-upon project parameters.

Selective perception is where we selectively interpret the behaviour of others based upon our particular interests, experiences and background.

Self-identity, also called self-concept, is our internal multi-faceted model and understanding of the 'self' as it relates to a number of characteristics such as gender, intellect, race, skills, abilities, competencies, physical characteristics and the personality we've identify for ourselves.

Self-fulfilling prophecy is a term used to describe the phenomenon where an individual works toward the validation of what they perceive, expect or believe.

Sidebar conversation is used to describe people are talking to each other and not paying attention during meetings.

Silo is a word used to depict the lack of cooperation, communication or common goals between departments in an organization, which results in a fragmented organization.

Situational leaders are leaders who flexes to the people, task and function that needs to be accomplished.

Small talk is an expression for any informal dialogue that has no functional purpose other than to generate interest in each other to continue having a conversation.

Stonewalling is a tactic that involves delaying or stalling proceedings, refusing to answer questions, or walking out on the discussion. It is intended to force you to give in, or at least feel intimidated enough to back off on some of the items in your proposal.

Therapeutic Rapport is created through the active demonstration of empathy and understanding by the coach, where the client then feels a sense of safety, trust and respect.

Values are important and enduring beliefs or ideals shared by the members of a culture or family about what is good or desirable and what is not. Values exert major influence on the behavior of an individual and serve as broad guidelines in all situations.

Virtual meetings are meeting where the parties are in different locations and use Internet based technology or video-conferencing or teleconference to connect.

Visual learners want information presented to them so that they can see it in order to learn.

Visualization is a mental technique that builds mental imagery to which your emotions and body responds. It will allow you to sit on your sofa and literally sense the situation as if it were real.

APPENDIX III

Bibliography

Amen, Daniel. 1998. *Change Your Brain, Change Your Life.* New York: Three Rivers Press.

Arbinger Institute, The. 2002. *Leadership and Self-Deception.* Barrett-Koehler San Francisco: Puslishers, Inc.

Bolton, Robert and Dorothy Grover Bolton. 2009. *People Styles at Work and Beyond, 2nd ed.* New York: Amacon.

Bonnstetter, Bill. 1993. *The Universal Language Disc.* Scottsdale: TTI, Ltd.

Carnegie, Dale. 1936. *How to Win Friends and Influence People.* New York: Simon & Schuster.

Cialdini, Robert. 2007. *Influence: the Psychology of Persuasion, revised edition.* New York: Harper Collins.

Darling, Diane. 2010. *The Networking Survival Guide, 2nd ed.* New York: MacGraw Hill.

Dimitrius, Jo-Ellan. 1999. *Reading People.* New York: Ballantine Books.

Fisher, Roger and William Ury. 1991. *Getting to Yes.* New York: Penguin Books.

Forward, Susan. 1997. *Emotional Blackmail.* New York: HarperCollins Publisher.

Gerstner Jr., Louis V. 2002. *Who Says Elephants Can't Dance?* New York: HarperCollins Publishers, Inc.

Goleman, Daniel. 2002. *Primal Leadership*. Boston: Havard Business School Press.

Goleman, Daniel. 1997. *Emotional Intelligence*. New York: Bantam Press.

Harvard Business Essentials. 2003. *Negotiation*. Boston: Harvard Business School Press.

Harvard Business Essentials. 2005. *Power, Influence and Persuasion*: Boston: Harvard Business School Press.

Hindle, Tim. 1998. *Negotiating Skills, Essential Managers*. New York: DK Publishing, Inc.

Kouzes, James M. and Barry Z. Posner. 2002. *Leadership Challenge, 3rd ed*. San Francisco: Jossey-Bass.

Langton, Nancy and Stephen P. Robbins. 2007. Organizational Behaviour Canadian 4th ed. Toronto: Pearson-Prentice Hall.

Latham, Gary P. 2009. *Becoming the Evidence-Based Manager*. Boston: Davies-Black

Mehrabian, Albert. 1971. *Implicit Communication of Emotions and Attitudes,* 2nd ed. Belmont, CA: Wadsworth.

Mintzberg, Henry.2009. *Managing*. San Francisco: Berrett-Koehler Publishers, In.

Rotman Magazine. Fall 2010. *It's Complicated*. Toronto: University of Toronto. Rotman Magazine. Winter 2011. *Thinking About Thinking II*. Toronto: University of Toronto.

Stone, Douglas, Bruce Patton, Sheila Heen. 2010. *Difficult Conversations, 10th anniversary edition*. New York: Penguin Books.

RECOMMENDED RESOURCES

Dynamic Communications
Dynamic Communication is a behaviorally-based communication seminar aimed at teaching people how to communicate using specialized techniques and methods to understand themselves and others. The seminar incorporates a behavioral assessment to give a more complete understanding of each individual. Participants learn how to interact with others and to appreciate each others' behavioral styles. Improved communication is noticed immediately after the seminar. *This workshop is certified for continuing educational credits.* The training is based upon the DISC Communication Model.

Team Building
This workshop is designed to enhance *team effectiveness*. You will be exposed to practical methodologies used to develop cohesive teams who communicate and work together in a more effective and productive manner. You will gain access to the most advanced, leading-edge skills for mobilizing cross-functional teams. Learn the reasons why teams fail and how to motivate individuals to work collaboratively by understanding the fundamental characteristics, communication styles and motivations of one another.

Leadership Development Program
This leadership program is made up of 12 workshops that cover subjects such as leadership styles, communication, conflict resolution, psychology of influence, decision-making, strategic planning, change management and more. Each participant will complete an online validated *Leadership Assessment* that outlines their core competencies, emotional intelligence, communication preferences and motivational factors. This program can be completed as integrated 12 modules or select stand-alone workshops.

"Selling with the Styles" Sales Intelligence Workshop
Learn proven strategies and techniques for developing more meaningful and professional sales relationships with your clients. Learn about you and your client's view of the world, how they choose to buy, how to build instant rapport, how to identify your client's buying/decision making strategies, and how to identify your client's motivational factors to manage your state of mind for peak performance.

Powerful Speaking and Presenting Skills
This course is designed for anyone who has to facilitate meetings, train or present to groups of people. Participants will discover the underlying factors that affect how individuals learn and what motivates them. You will gain knowledge about communication techniques, learning strategies, special listening skills and how to capture and maintain the attention of your audience. Training includes experiential exercises, lectures, demonstration and self-assessment surveys.

Assessment Profiles
Assessment profiles are available for communication styles, leadership preferences, sales / job competencies, relationship styles, emotional intelligence and motivation factors.

Keynote Speaking Engagements
Claudia Ferryman is a highly sought-after keynote speaker. Her message conveys the perfect blend of conceptual and practical strategies. Claudia utilizes passion and humour to engage the audience. She has been a keynote guest speaker for numerous corporations and not-for-profit organizations. Participants are known to leave workshops saying *"That was the best presentation I've ever attended!"*

To reserve Claudia Ferryman or book one of these workshops for your next event, email info@rainmakerstrategies.org or call 1-416-410-1614.

ABOUT THE AUTHOR

Claudia Ferryman is a renowned keynote speaker and sought-after consultant with over 20 years experience and expertise in organizational psychology, communication, influence and persuasion, and change management. She is CEO of Rainmaker Strategies Group and an instructor at the University of Toronto, where she has received the Award of Excellence in Teaching.

She has worked with corporations such as Rogers, Motorola, Kodak, Bell, Rotman School of Management, CIBC, Moneris Solutions (Bank of Montreal/Royal Bank joint venture), as well as government ministries, boards of education and multiple non-profit and community service groups to solve difficult organizational problems by guiding them on what has been described as an engaging, fast-paced and experiential journey inside the deeper psychological motivations that drive behaviour.

Claudia enjoys taking complex concepts and presenting them in ways that are easy to understand and apply. She has improved the performance and productivity of numerous teams by imparting powerful techniques on how to get better results through leveraging communication in a wide range of professional contexts. She holds a degree in organizational psychology and multiple certifications in NLP and behavioural/values analysis.

Made in the USA
Charleston, SC
17 September 2011